FOREWORD

The 17th John Moores Liverpool Exhibition has, as always, been sponsored by Sir John himself through his Family Trust, and the Trustees of NMGM and I are delighted at this continued support. For us, the exhibition is one of the chief events on our calendar. We particularly value its capacity to encourage debate, to attract a wide audience from far afield, and to stimulate the young.

I am very grateful to this year's jury, Lewis Biggs, Maurice Cockrill, John Hoyland and Jayne Purdy. They have selected a show whose accent is on catholicity and power of artistic imagination. Their choice for first prize, Andrzej Jackowski's 'The Beekeeper's Son', is a haunting and poetical image far removed from the more conceptually inclined winners of recent exhibitions.

Although there are many fresh faces in this John Moores, as there should be, one of the features of the show is the presence of a number of Britain's most widely respected 'elder statesmen'. I am delighted by their renewed support for the show, for although the exhibition is often seen as being the preserve of the up and coming, its real strength lies in its power to command interest and loyalty from the widest possible spectrum of artists.

I would like to thank my colleagues at the Walker Art Gallery: Julian Treuherz, Keeper of Art Galleries, and particularly Alex Kidson, Assistant Curator of Fine Art, who has undertaken in full the organisation of the exhibition. For their special assistance to Alex my thanks go to Shirley McArdle; Val Evans in Design and Jim Hendry and John Reddish in the Property Department. I should also like to pay tribute to Bill Mansfield, Chief Technician at the Walker, whose last John Moores before retirement this is. He has worked on every exhibition in the series since the second, in 1959, and his efforts and unfailing good humour have been a continued source of inspiration for generations of gallery staff - not to mention jurors and artists themselves.

Richard Foster,
Director
National Museums and Galleries on Merseyside

SPONSORS

The Exhibition is sponsored jointly by Sir John Moores CBE and the Trustees of the National Museums and Galleries on Merseyside, of which the Walker Art Gallery forms part.

CONDITIONS OF ENTRY

The exhibition was open to all living artists working in the U.K. Entrants were limited to one painting - preferably new - in an accepted modern medium, which was designed to hang on a wall and to project no more than six inches. Sculpture, watercolours and graphics were excluded. The paintings entered were placed before a jury who selected the exhibition and awarded the prizes.

SALE OF WORKS

Most of the paintings are for sale. Prices are available on application at the desk or from the Exhibition Secretary, through whom purchases may be negotiated. No commission is charged.

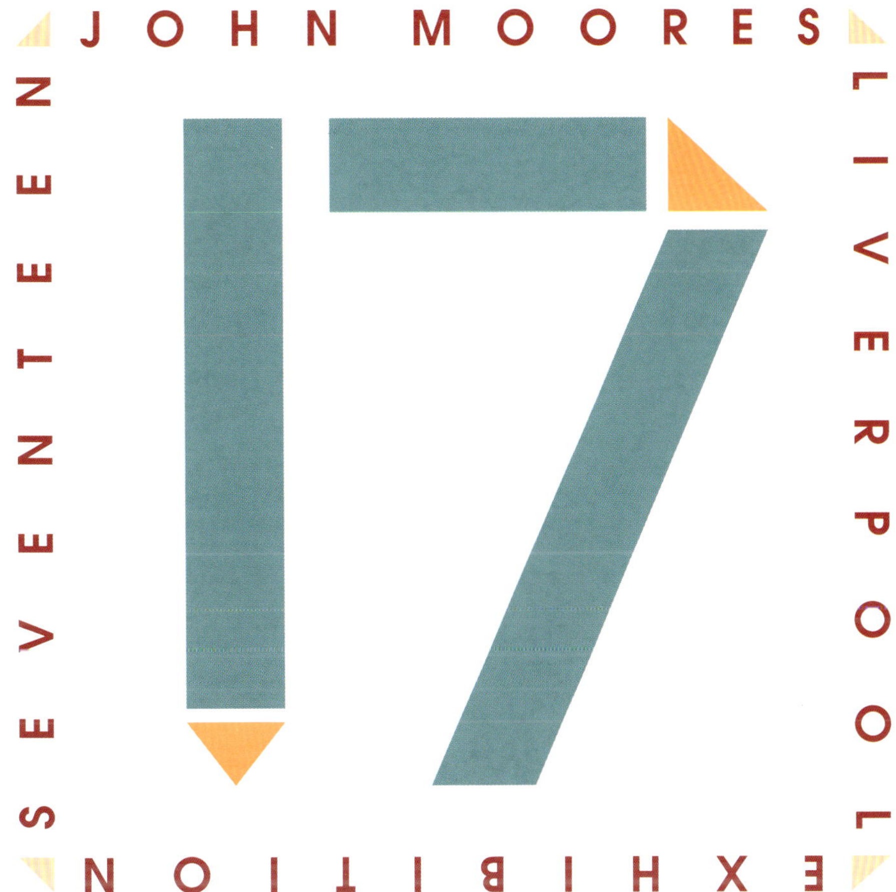

WALKER · ART · GALLERY · LIVERPOOL
18 OCTOBER 1991 · 19 JANUARY 1992

MONDAY to SATURDAY 10AM - 5PM SUNDAY 12NOON - 5PM
CLOSED 24 - 26 DECEMBER & 1 JANUARY

PRIZEWINNERS

1st Prize *(£20,000 purchase)*

Andrzej Jackowski

£1,000 Prizes

James Brook
John Capstack
Jeff Dellow
Arturo Di Stefano
Stephen Farthing
Nichollas Hamper
Andrea Lansley
Adam Lowe
Jock McFadyen
Michael Simpson

PREVIOUS 1st PRIZEWINNERS

1957	Jack Smith *(Open Prize)*
1959	Patrick Heron *(Main Prize)*
1961	Henry Mundy *(Open Prize)*
1963	Roger Hilton *(Open Prize)*
1965	Michael Tyzack *(Open Prize)*
1967	David Hockney
1969	Richard Hamilton
	Mary Martin *(joint winners of The Main Prize)*
1972	Euan Uglow
1974	Myles Murphy
1976	John Walker
1978	Noel Forster
1980	Michael Moon
1982	John Hoyland
1985	Bruce McLean
1987	Tim Head
1989	Lisa Milroy

JURY

John Hoyland
Jayne Purdy
Lewis Biggs
Maurice Cockrill

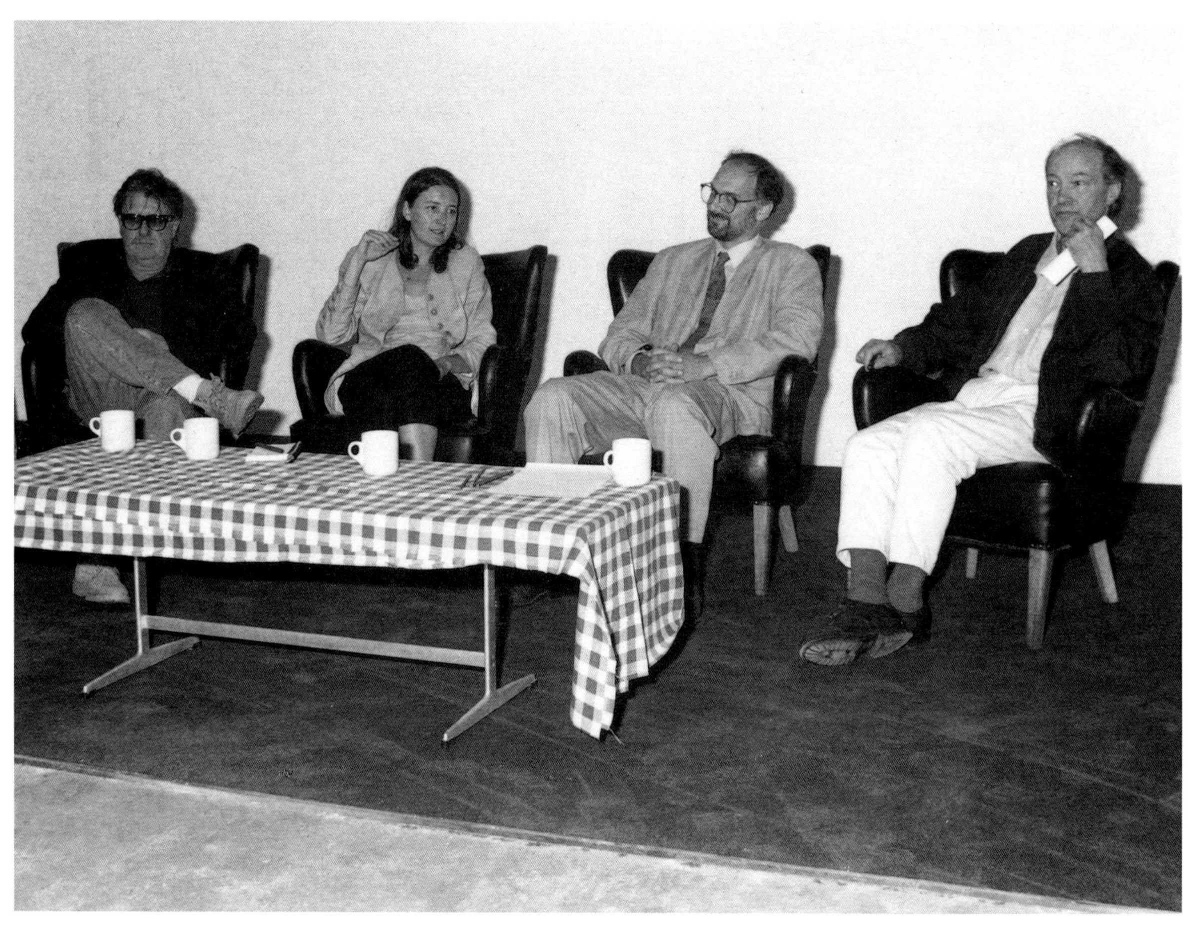

CATALOGUE

All the artists were invited to write a few words about the exhibited work for publication in this catalogue.

Some asked that their picture be allowed to stand alone, with no accompanying statement.

Height precedes width in all measurements.

ANDRZEJ JACKOWSKI
THE BEEKEEPER'S SON

oil on canvas   168 x 233.5cm

FIRST PRIZEWINNER

The image of *The Beekeeper's Son* has evolved slowly over the last year - though it's terrain I've explored over several years. It's a rich terrain full of desire and fear, intimacy and distance, dark flesh and dead fruit.

Andrzej Jackowski was born in 1947 in Penley, North Wales. He studied at Camberwell School of Art 1966-69, Falmouth School of Art 1972-73 and the Royal College of Art 1974-77. While still a student he exhibited *Room With Exposure* in John Moores 10, 1976 which was purchased by the University of Liverpool. He also showed in John Moores 12 and 13, 1980 and '82. Since 1982 he has had one-man shows in London (Moira Kelly Fine Art 1982, Anne Berthoud 1984, Marlborough Fine Art 1986 and '89) and Liverpool and Manchester (both touring). Recent exhibitions include *The Tree of Life*, South Bank Centre 1989 in which he won a prize, and *Modern Painters*, Manchester City Art Gallery 1991.

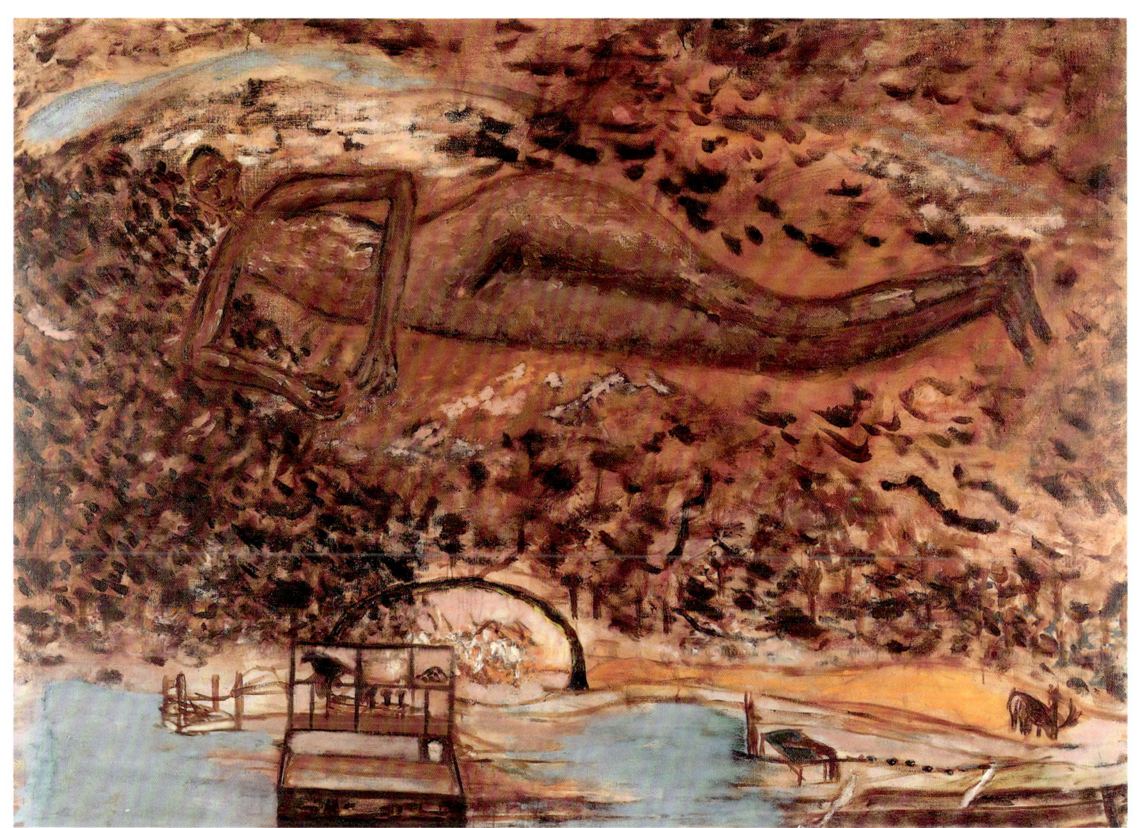

JAMES BROOK
WATER

oil on canvas with fabric   127.5 x 183 cm

PRIZEWINNER

As source material for this work I have used tele-vision and magazine photographs. The nature of the paint seems to remove the bodies of the sol-diers from the confines of their photo-chemical cell and re-invent them organically. This revelation is then partially denied by wrapping the painting in a blue sequined net. But the net also creates a feel-ing of nearness at distance, of intimacy and exclu-sion. Its function has been subverted from that of a fashion-fabric with built-in obsolescence and instead it is given an active pictorial role. It is as transient as the presence of the soldiers. Its flicker-ing surface complements the representational nature of the work whilst at the same time con-tributing to the pervading sense of artifice.

James Brook was born in Huddersfield in 1959. He studied at Exeter College of Art 1981-84 and held a one-man show at the Red Herring Gallery Brighton in 1986 before resuming his studies at Chelsea School 1989-90. Recent shows include the London Group 1989, Riverside One 1990 (in which he was a prizewinner) and *New Contemporaries* (Arnolfini Bristol and touring) 1990-91.

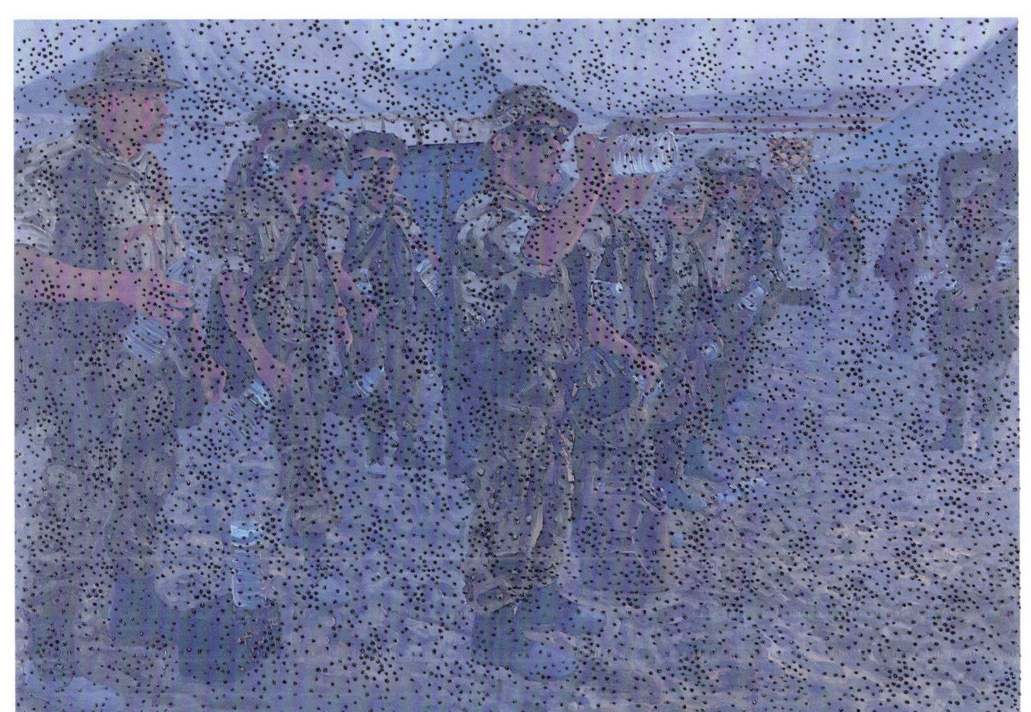

JOHN CAPSTACK
EXPULSION NO. II

oil on canvas   269 x 366 cm

PRIZEWINNER

My work is figurative and is concerned with reflections on man and his environment and symbols.

John Capstack was born in Halifax, West Yorkshire in 1957. He studied at Percival Whitley College Halifax 1975-77 and at Manchester Polytechnic 1977-80. In 1990 he held one-man shows at Dean Clough, Halifax and at the Young Unknowns Gallery, London and this year was included in the East National Open Art Exhibition, Norwich.

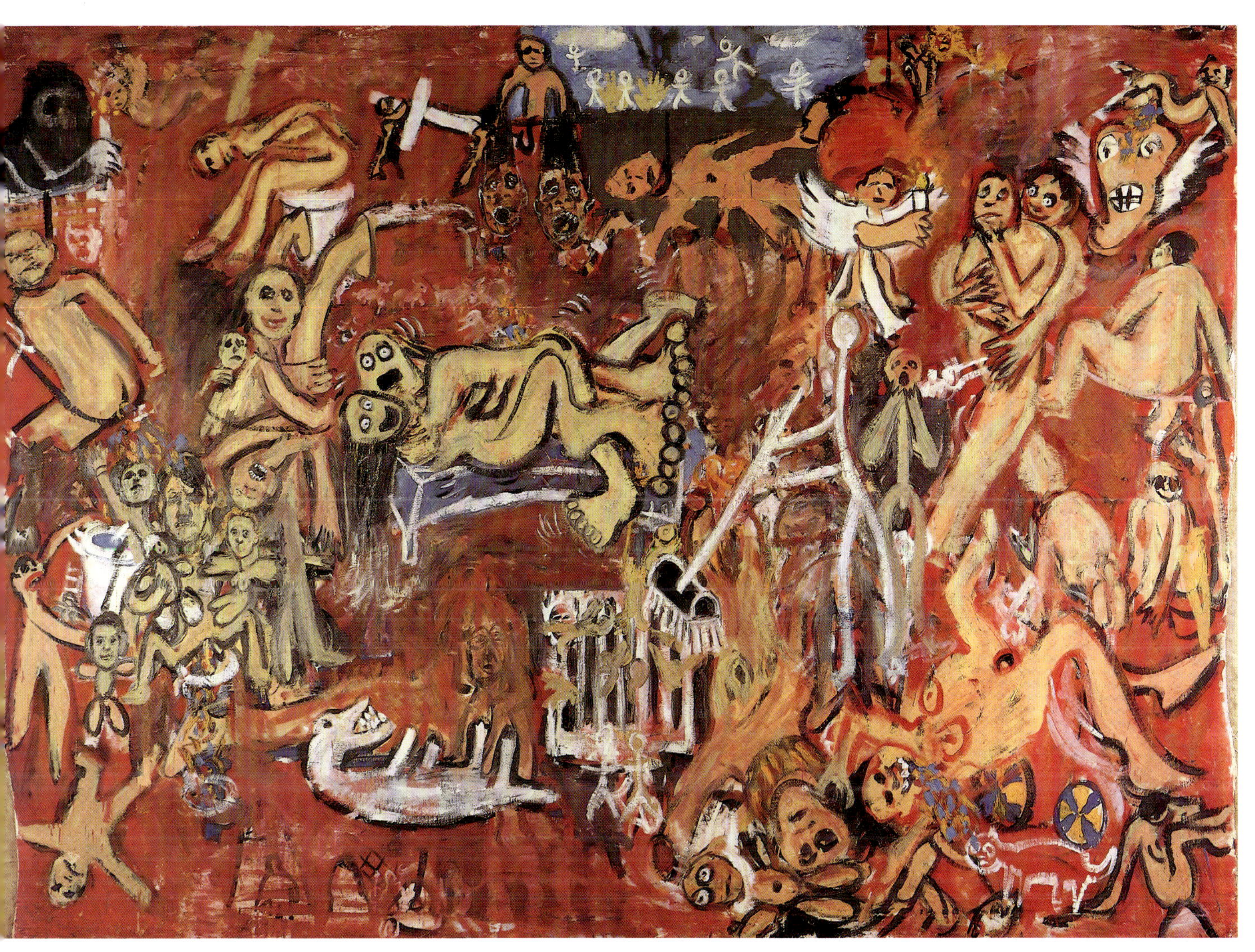

JEFF DELLOW
AFRICA: SEED AND SHADOW

acrylic on canvas   171.5 x 220.5cm

PRIZEWINNER

During a recent visit to Zimbabwe, made with the assistance of the British Council, I attended an artist's workshop Pachipanwe (the Shona word for 'meeting together') where artists from neighbouring African states and other countries met to work and share experience. A response to this and the character of the place has been a positive focus in my recent work.

This painting involves the idea of a paradise under threat; the precariousness of a world of potential - through a natural strength of form and fertility - faced by cultural and political forces of exploitation.

ITEMS OF NOTE OR FASCINATION; ZIMBABWE, SEPTEMBER 16 - OCTOBER 1 1990:

People:
from Zambia, Zimbabwe, Mozambique, S. Africa, Botswana, USA, Finland, New Zealand.
Natural Forms:
large insects, seeds, birds, bees/hornets, wildlife.
Man-made Forms:
sculpture, bushmen paintings on rock, territorial decoration on housing and huts.
Mass-Produced Forms:
recycled paper, grass, plastic, 1960s taxis, rarity of Walkmans.

Jeff Dellow was born in Newcastle-upon-Tyne in 1949. He studied at St Martin's School of Art 1968-69, Maidstone College of Art 1969-71 and the Slade 1972-74, followed by a Cheltenham Fellowship 1974-75. One of his earliest group shows was John Moores 10, 1976 and he has since exhibited regularly in London and nationwide. Since his second appearance in the John Moores in 1989 his shows have included *Art 90* and *Art 91* (Business Design Centre Islington), *Creative Assets,* Harris Art Gallery Preston 1990; Todd Gallery London 1990, *Pachipanwe III,* National Gallery of Zimbabwe, Harare, and the 1991 Whitechapel Open.

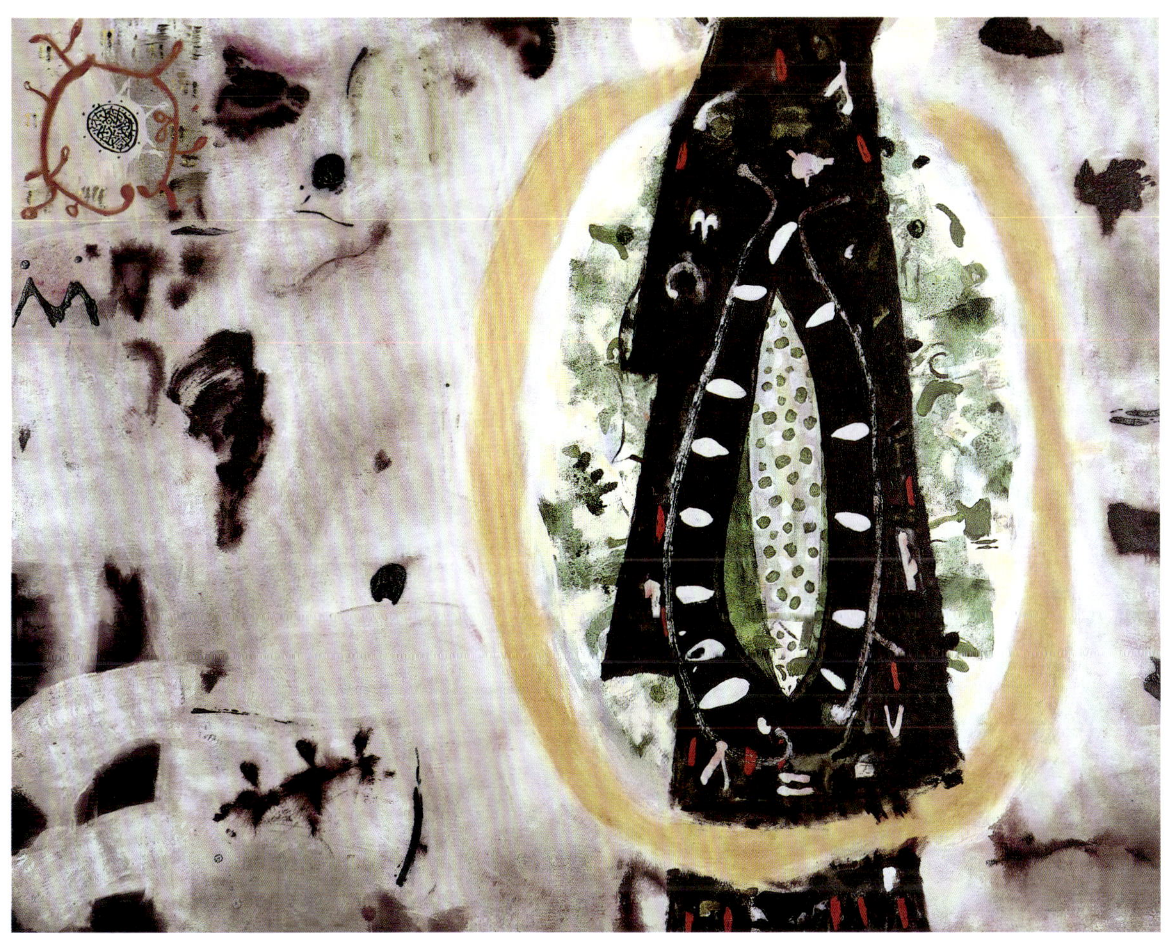

ARTURO DI STEFANO
ST PAUL DE MAUSOLE

oil and wax on linen   208 x 145.5 cm

PRIZEWINNER

St Paul de Mausole is the name of the asylum in St Rémy de Provence where Van Gogh stayed from 8th May 1889 to 16th May 1890. The picture depicts the cloisters of the priory adjoining the asylum. Painting this picture was a way of thinking about his life and work, of remembering him as one would an absent relative or friend.

Arturo Di Stefano was born in 1955 and brought up in Liverpool, where he did his Foundation year at the Polytechnic 1973-74. He moved to London to study at Goldsmiths' College 1974-77 and the Royal College of Art 1978-81. His first one-man exhibition in 1985 was followed by a year's Italian Government Scholarship to study at the Accademia Albertina in Turin. He has since held a number of one-man shows, most recently at Pomeroy Purdy Gallery London 1989, 1991; at Eastbourne Clark Gallery Florida 1989, and Helmut Pabst, Frankfurt 1991. The Walker Art Gallery is to hold a one-man show of his work in January 1993.

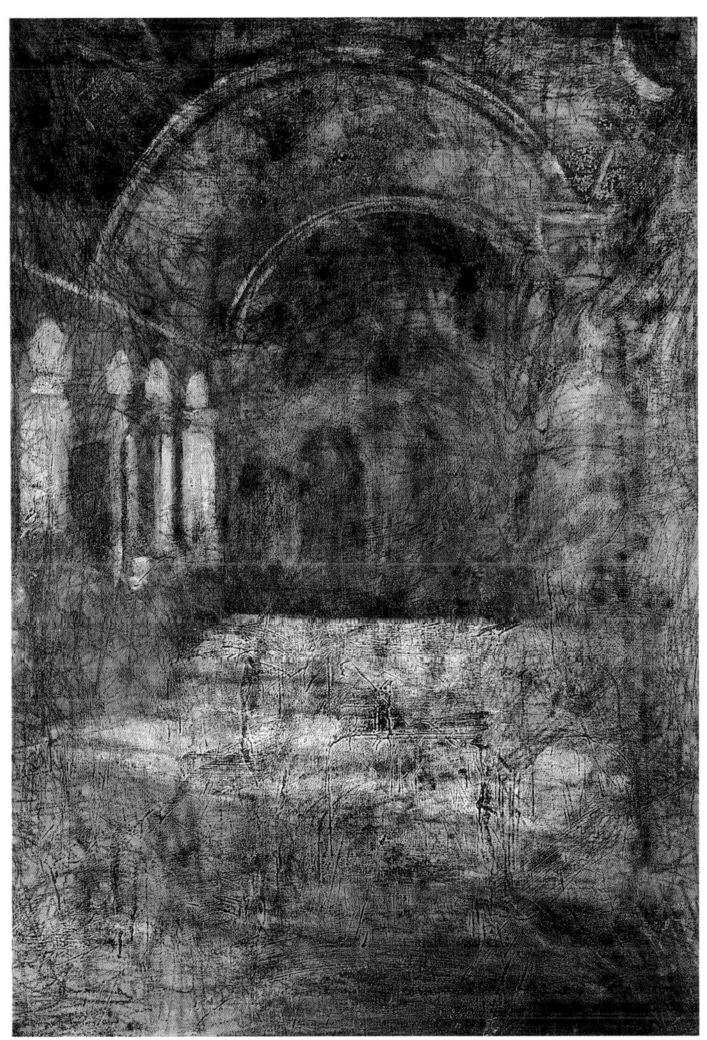

STEPHEN FARTHING
THE KNOWLEDGE

oil on canvas   173 x 330 cm

PRIZEWINNER

The Knowledge is the licensing examination taken by London taxi drivers. It tests their memory of the streets.

Painted in oils over an airbrush drawing in acrylic, *The Knowledge* is an experiment. The aim was to see what a city would look like taken indoors. In this painting both the city and the room are inventions, but both are based on drawings and photographs made in Latin America during 1990.

Stephen Farthing was born in London in 1950. He studied at St Martin's School of Art 1969-73 and at the Royal College of Art 1973-76; he was Abbey Major Scholar at the British School in Rome 1975-76. One of his student paintings, *Louis XV Rigaud*, won a prize in John Moores 10, 1976 and was purchased by the Walker Art Gallery. His work has been seen regularly in Liverpool: in six subsequent John Moores; Peter Moores Liverpool Project 5 1979; *The Construction of a Monument*, Bluecoat Gallery 1982 and most recently in *Mute Accomplices*, a one-man retrospective organised by the Museum of Modern Art, Oxford, 1987-88. Recent major exhibitions have included *Stephen Farthing and the Leonardo Exhibition*, QEH London 1989 and a number of shows in Brazil, Uruguay and Mexico, 1990-91. The exhibition *The Knowledge* was shown earlier this year in the Palacio Municipal, Montevideo, Uruguay and an installation of the same title will be seen this autumn at the Spacex Gallery Exeter. Stephen Farthing is currently Ruskin Master of Drawing at Oxford University and Professorial Fellow at St. Edmund Hall.

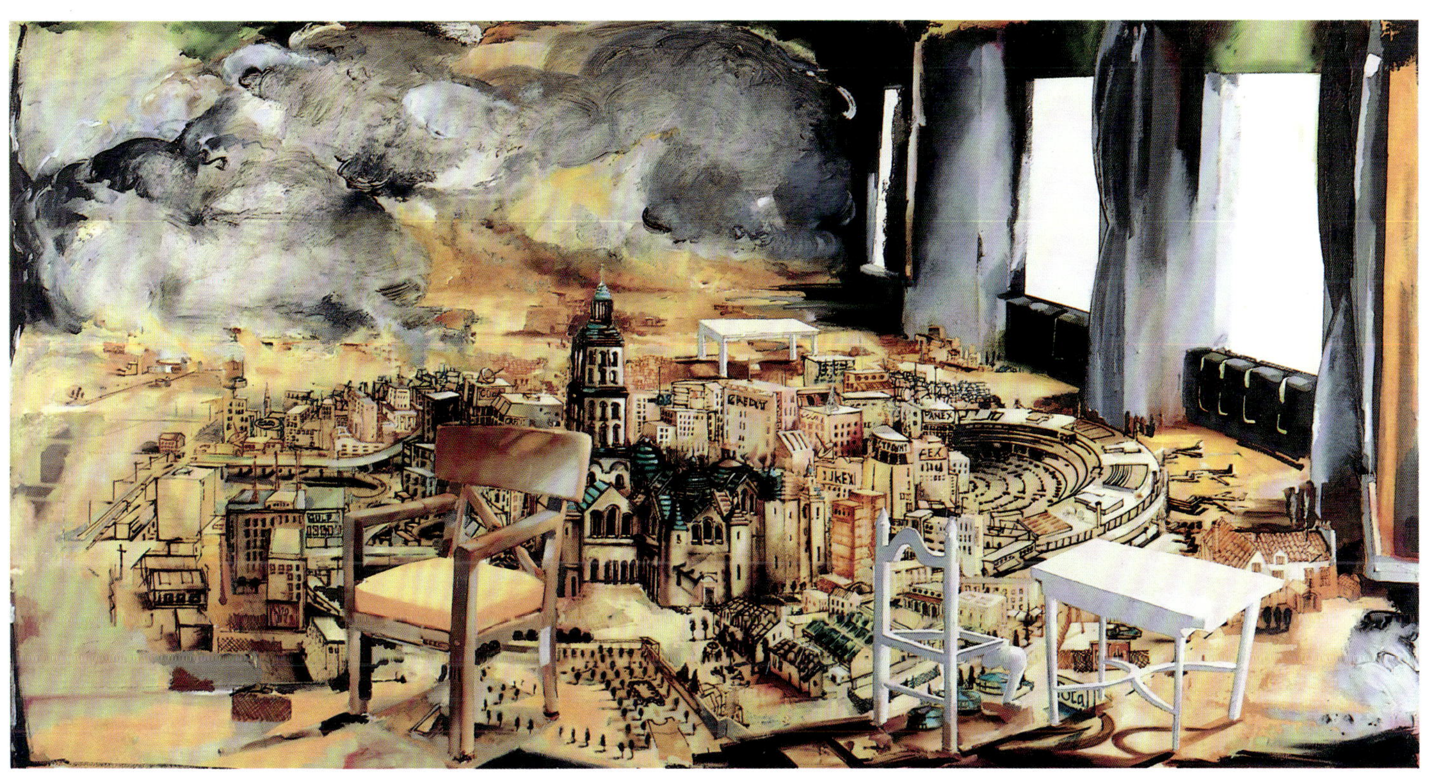

NICHOLLAS HAMPER
THE INTERVENTION OF THE DONER KEBAB

hammerite, enamel, bitumen   240 x 178 cm
and car spray on canvas

PRIZEWINNER

Forms of nature, mechanical forms and food forms are metamorphosed into severe sculpture-like presences. The overall colour might be developed from a motor manufacturer's colour chart, combined with the colours found in photos in glossy cookery books and on the menus in hamburger bars. The intention is to link the contemporary and the technological with that which is edible; the hard with the soft; the efficiency of commercial usefulness with the craving for fast food.

Nichollas Hamper was born at Chatham, Kent in 1956. He studied at the Slade School 1975-79 and at the Royal College of Art 1980-82. He has had one-man shows at Fischer Fine Art 1985 and Rex Irwin, Sydney 1984 and '86 and more recently in Oxford at Oxford Polytechnic and Ruskin School *(Fast Food Subversive)* 1990. Recent group shows include Tolly Cobbold 5, 1985; the CAS Art Market, Smith's Gallery 1985-88; *Metropolis*, Raab Gallery London 1988 and *Three Ways*, British Council to Eastern Europe 1990. He taught at Oxford Polytechnic 1988-91 and is currently visiting lecturer at the Ruskin School of Drawing.

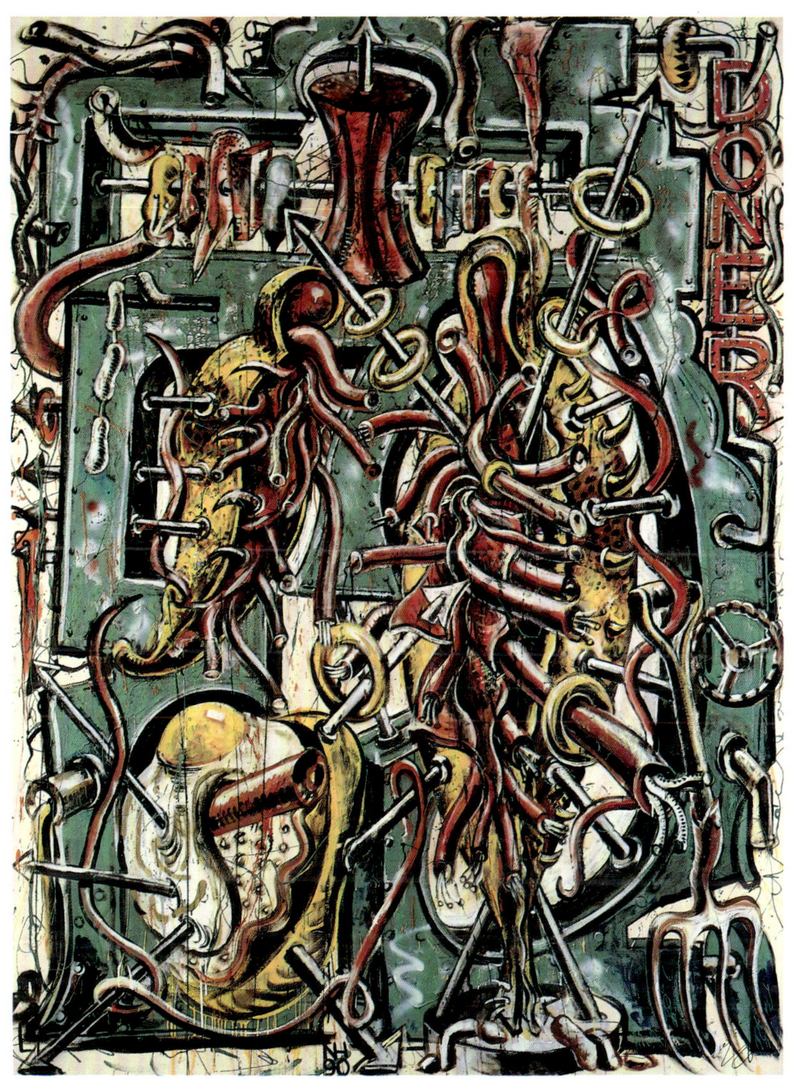
DONER

ANDREA LANSLEY
SELF-PORTRAIT

oil on canvas   256 x 180.5 cm

PRIZEWINNER

This work belongs to a series in which I attempt to reclaim my physical history and re-assert it in my own terms. In this painting I have transformed the perceptions of others, and their subsequent effect on my own self-image, into a tangible form. By objectifying sensation in this way, I hope both to intimidate and to interrogate the viewer.

For me the painting also retains elements of humour in its irony. However, inevitably and most importantly, it is about being a woman as experienced, not defined.

Andrea Lansley was born in Manchester in 1960. She studied at Wirral College of Art and Design 1987-88 and at Liverpool Polytechnic 1988-91. As a student prizewinner at Wirral College she held a one-person show at the Williamson Art Gallery Birkenhead in 1988; her work has subsequently been seen in the Whitworth Young Contemporaries 1989, Threshers' *Artistic Licence,* University of Liverpool 1990, '91, the *Fresh Art Fair,* Islington 1991 and in group shows in Liverpool.

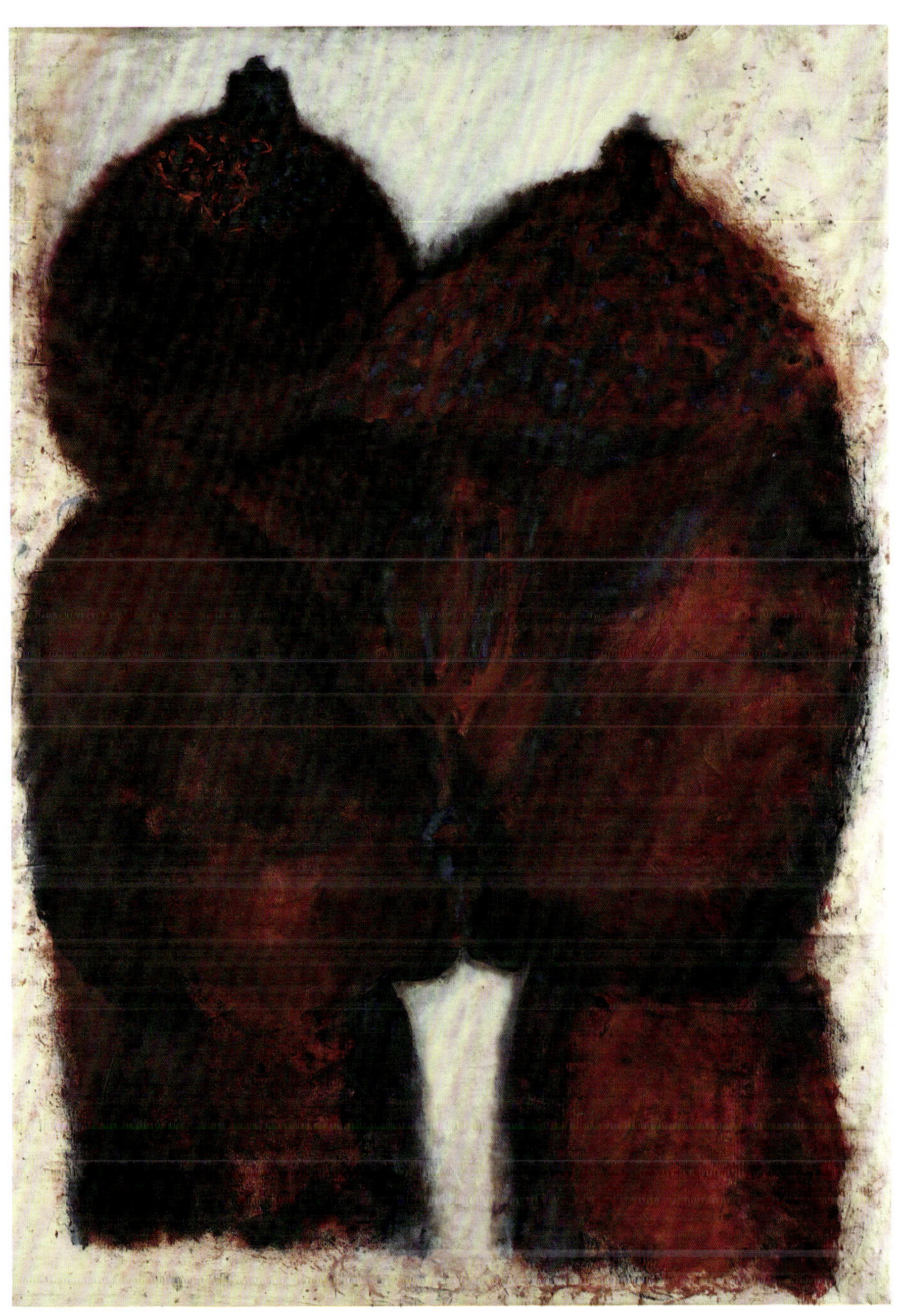

ADAM LOWE
THE HOMELY PROTESTANT

oil and epoxy resin on canvas   180.5 x 333 cm

PRIZEWINNER

The Homely Protestant was painted over a four-month period and finished this July. In content and appearance it changed many times as it was being made, each departure a response to what preceded it. The result is a work that is neither figurative nor abstract, although issues of figuration and abstraction hardly seem relevant. More fruitful might be a distinction between *conceptual* and *non-conceptual* attitudes towards content. Simply, conceptualists place themselves, apparently objectively, outside the work and comment from this localised vantage point. Non-conceptualists, acknowledging the limitations and likely errors involved in 'understanding', follow a series of cognitive trails in an advance towards meaning which is continually developing and being updated.

The Homely Protestant has a complex, even contradictory pictorial space, but hopefully, like a Turk's Head knot, its seamlessness denies a dominantly analytical appraisal. The resin appendages interrupt the surface and act as an obstacle which you have to look past.

The title refers to an important painting by Robert Motherwell. His obituary appeared in the paper the morning I was completing the entry form for this competition. It seemed appropriate.

Adam Lowe was born in 1959 in Oxford, where he studied at the Ruskin School 1978-81 before moving to the Royal College of Art 1982-85. His exhibitions include *Prelude*, Kettle's Yard Cambridge 1985, Smiths Gallery London 1986, and one-man shows at Pomeroy Purdy 1989 and '91. His five prints *Surface Mapping* and related works will be shown at Marrs Gallery Tokyo 1992.

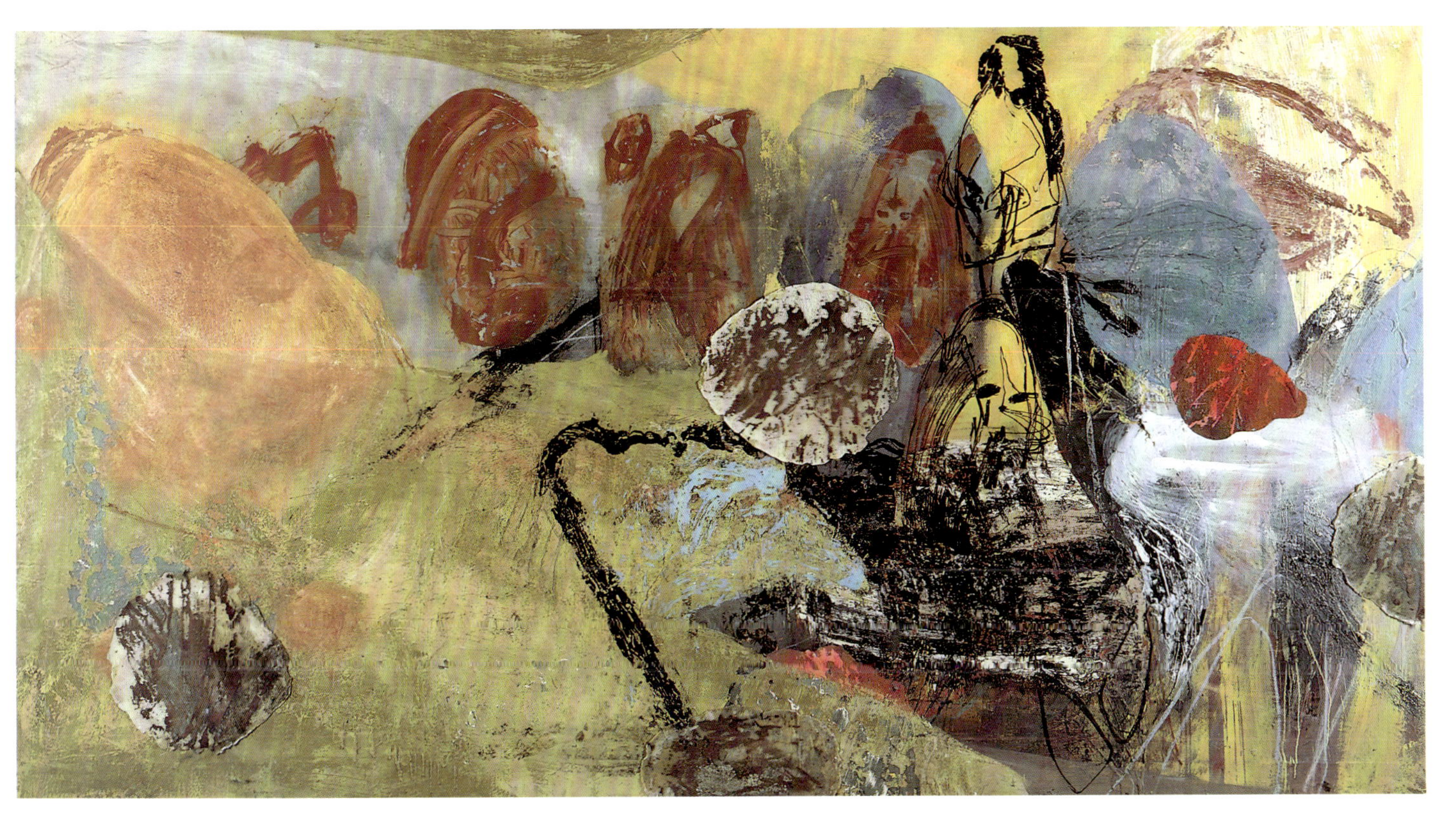

JOCK McFADYEN
ASTOR PLACE

oil on canvas   194 x 160.5 cm

PRIZEWINNER

My picture is of Astor Place subway station in New York. As I get older I seem to be making more pictures about places than of people.

This picture reflects that, and feels like my memory of being there.

Jock McFadyen was born in Paisley, Scotland, in 1950. He studied at Chelsea School of Art 1973-77. His first one-man show was at ACME Gallery London 1978. He was Artist-in-Residence at the National Gallery 1981-82. His most recent one-man shows have been at the Ceolfrith Gallery Sunderland (and tour) 1986, Scottish Gallery London 1989, William Jackson Gallery London 1991 and the Imperial War Museum London 1991, which tours to Glasgow and Manchester 1992. This is his second appearance in the John Moores exhibition, the first having been in 1980.

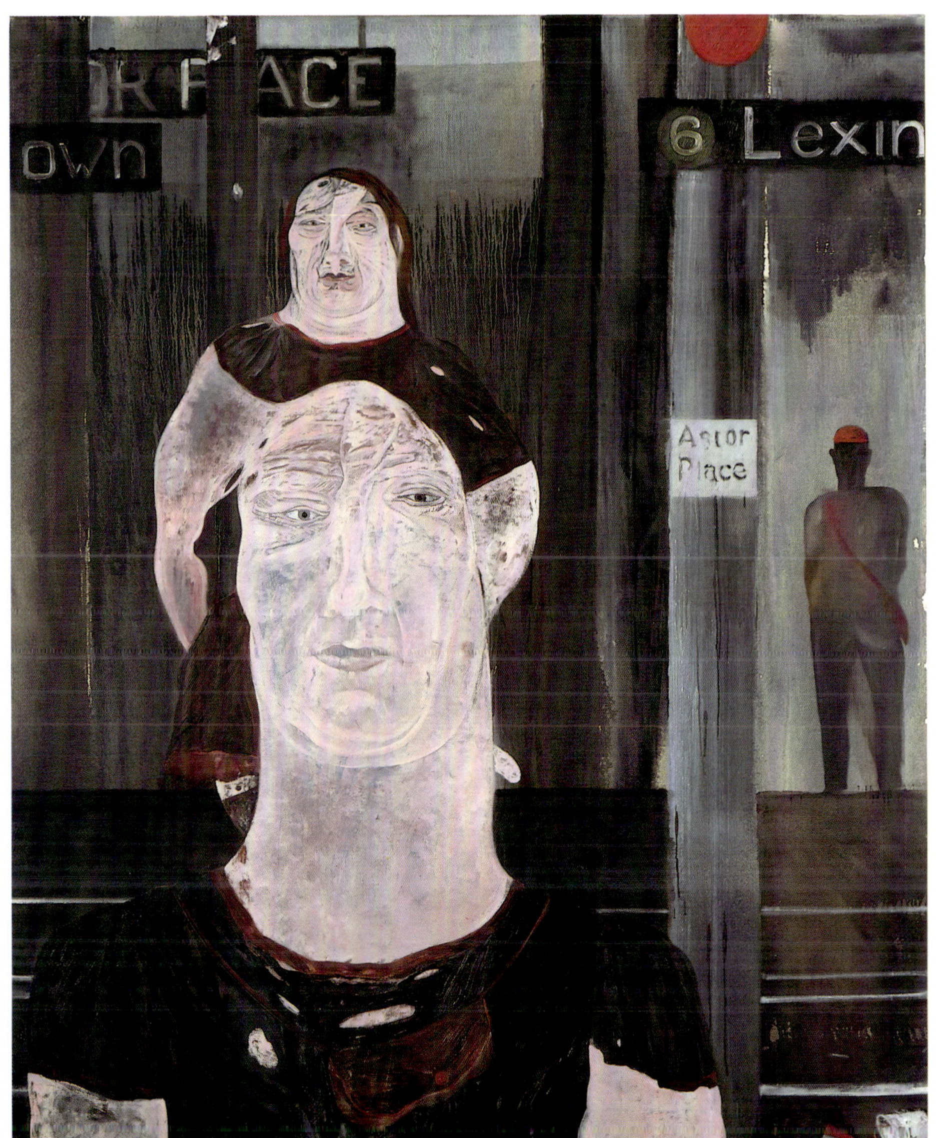
OR PLACE
own
6 Lexin
Astor
Place

MICHAEL SIMPSON
TENIR EN LAISSE

oil on canvas   254 x 366.5 cm

PRIZEWINNER

I began working on *Tenir en Laisse* in December 1990. It was completed by early July of this year.

Its origins go back to the mid-70s when I bought three Gallimard paperbacks from the series *La Realité Dépasse La Fiction* by Albert Aycard and Jacqueline Frank. They were illustrated photographic documents of the absurd; mostly signs, hoardings, advertisements, full of the evidence of human stupidity. One volume contained the image *Tenir en Laisse:* the manicured poodle.

This curious metaphor was for me immediately implicit - politically familiar. But the idea needed time to germinate; it was still only a fragment. The process of finding the source and inventing its context, however long it takes, epitomises the way in which I work.

Despite the subjective appearance of the painting, once its skeptic theme was established, my main concerns throughout were formal, particularly regarding colour and the aberrant, mischievous qualities of the pink.

From the outset I must have re-painted the pink a hundred times, without ever quite finding the subtle coherency I was after.

Michael Simpson was born in Dorset in 1940. He studied at Bournemouth College of Art 1958-60 and the Royal College of Art 1960-63. His first one-man show in 1964 was at the Piccadilly Gallery, where further shows took place in 1968 and 1972. He shared first prize in the Northern Ireland Arts Council Open in 1968 and at the Tolly Cobbold, Cambridge in 1977. More recent shows include *British Drawing*, Hayward Gallery 1982; one-man shows at the Arnolfini, Bristol 1983 and the Serpentine Gallery 1986; *On a Plate*, Serpentine Gallery 1987, and John Moores 16, 1989. He is currently associate lecturer in painting at Bath College of Higher Education.

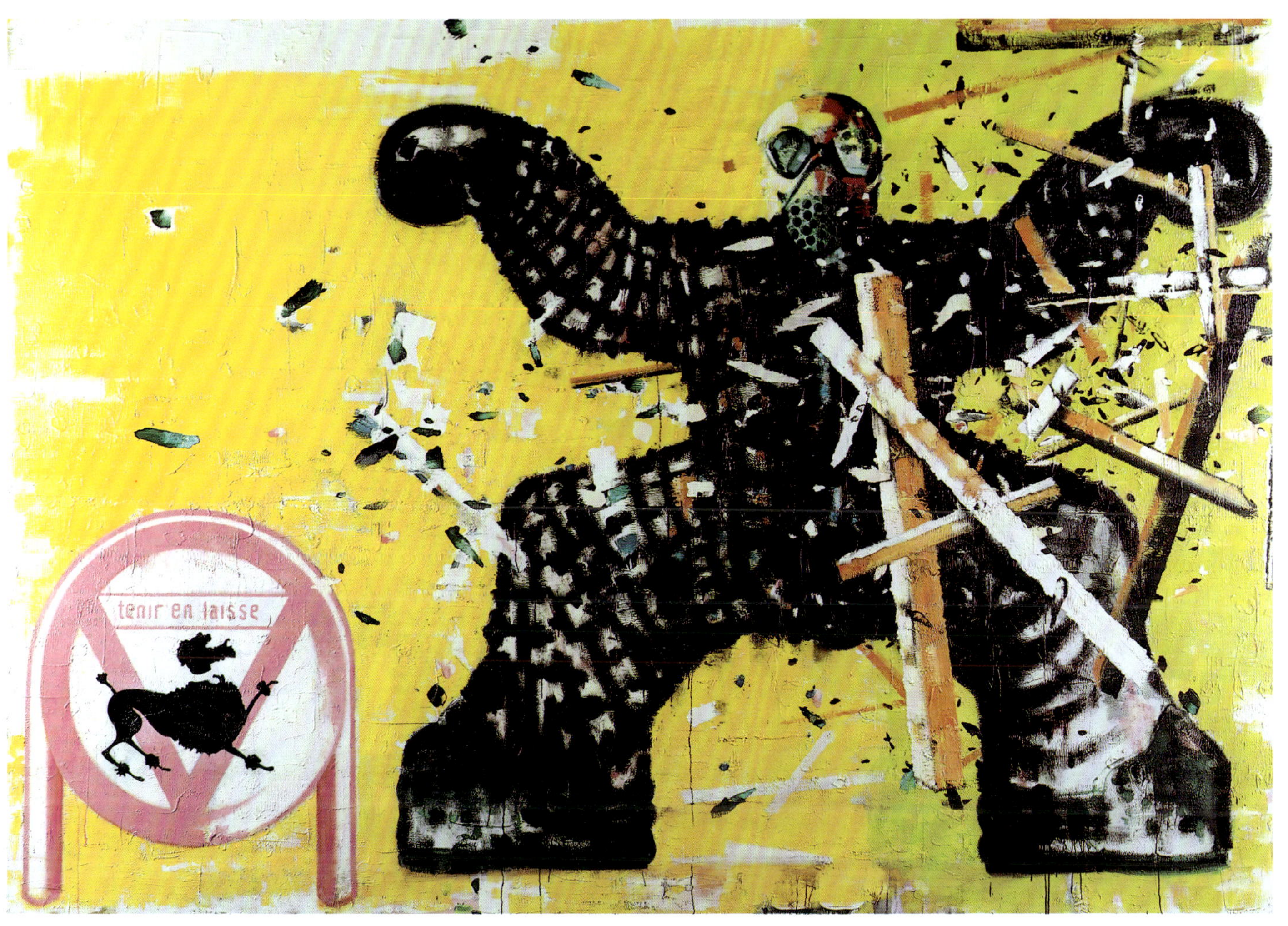
tenir en laisse

WILL ADAMS
PARROT AND TIGER DREAM

oil on canvas   182 x 122.5 cm

As the title suggests, the starting point for this painting was a dream. Whilst realising its disturbing, fearful nature, I have come to look on it with affection and humour. The force of the tiger and the wise foolishness of the parrot began to seem like positive qualities in most of us.

For me this work has marked a new approach in my painting.

Will Adams was born in Hunstanton, Norfolk, in 1951. He studied at the Fine Art Department, University of Reading 1969-74. His first one-man exhibition was at the 57 Gallery, Edinburgh in 1975. He has appeared in four Whitechapel Opens and showed in the Whitechapel's *Art for Society* 1978. In the mid 1980s he held a series of community-based residencies in the East End of London and his one-man show *Ten People* appeared at Camerawork, London 1984. He has appeared in several recent exhibitions in London and is currently working on a mural, 'Conference of the Birds', for a new primary school in Bethnal Green.

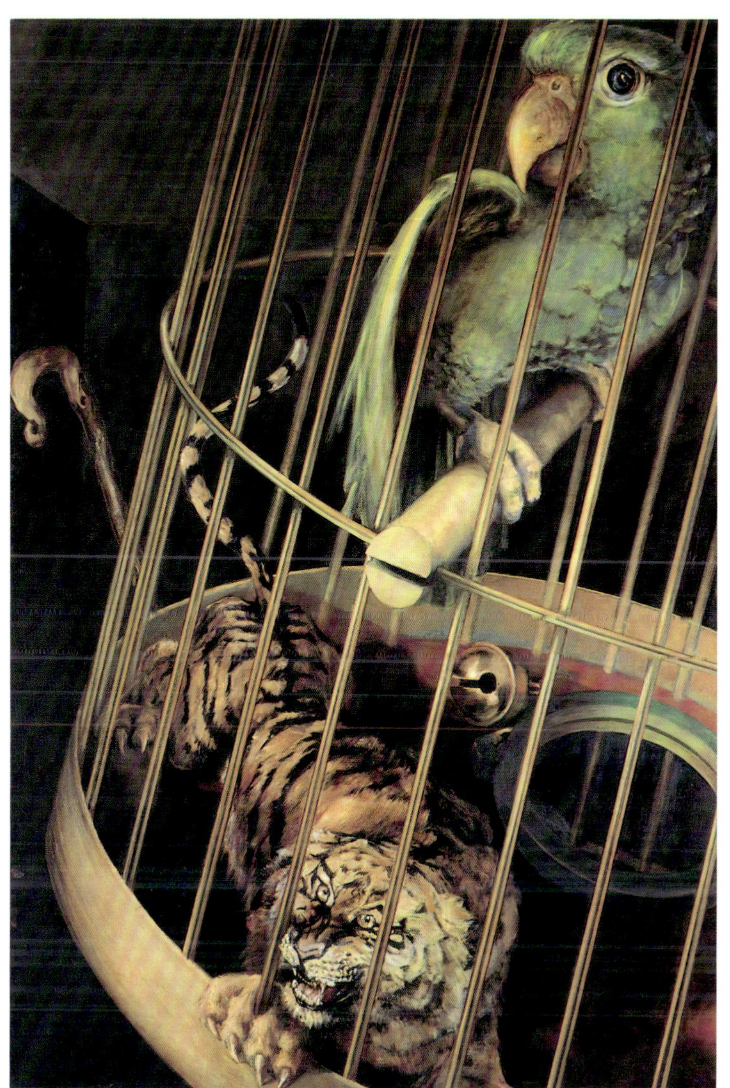

BASIL BEATTIE
ANOTHER TIME, ANOTHER PLACE

oil and wax on flax   259 x 305cm

The title *Another Time, Another Place* suggests temporal, geographical and perhaps psychological changes. Reflecting on these factors provided me with a background for this painting.

Basil Beattie was born in Hartlepool in 1935. He studied at West Hartlepool College of Art 1950-56 and at the Royal Academy Schools 1958-61. His first one-man show was at the Greenwich Theatre Gallery in London in 1968 since when he has exhibited widely in London, his native North-East and abroad. He has showed in four previous John Moores, winning second prize with *Pathfinder* in 1989. In 1991 he has been represented at the Chicago International Art Exposition, the Basel Art Fair, and the Goldsmiths' College Centenary, and his installation *Drawing on the Interior* will be seen at the Eagle Gallery, Farringdon, London. Basil Beattie lectures at Goldsmiths' College.

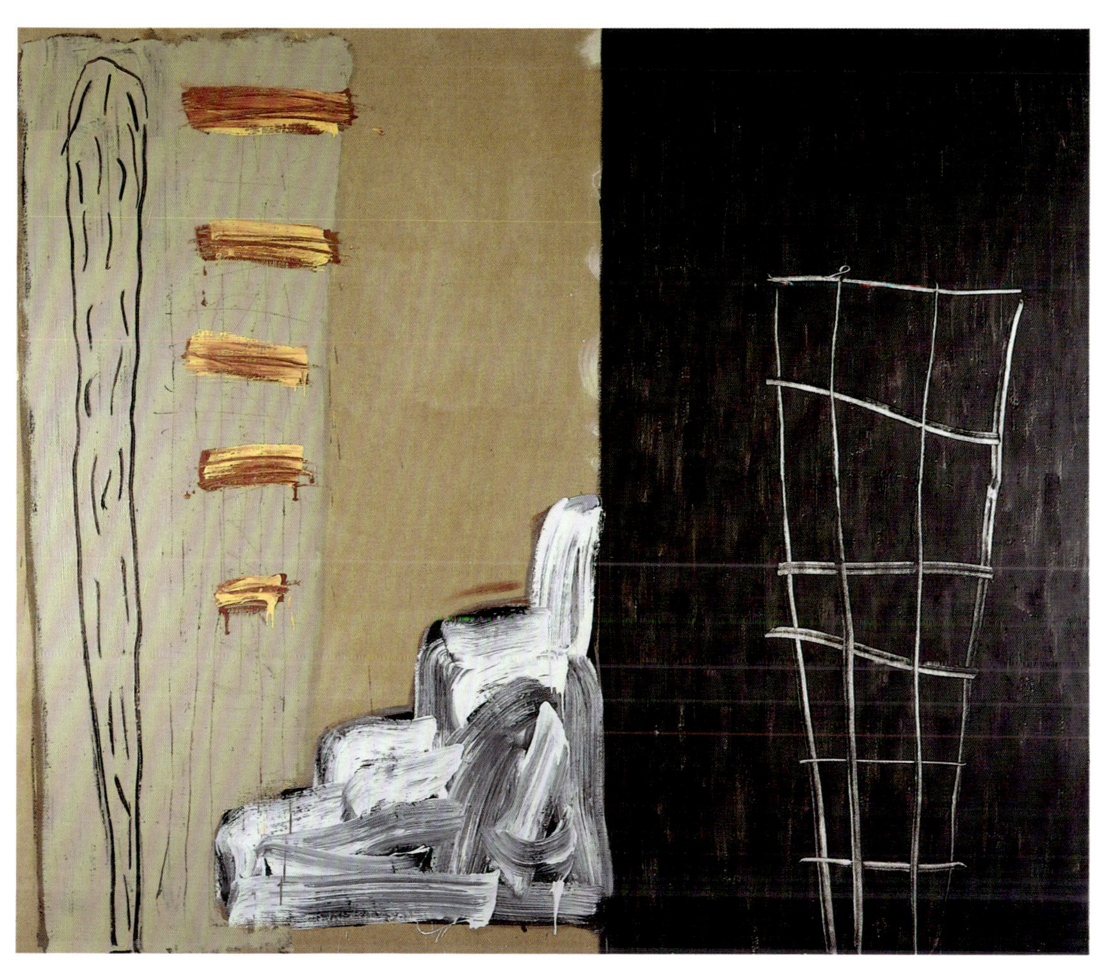

JOHN BICKNELL
UNTITLED

oil on canvas   202.5 x 330 cm

The particular warm red ochre of this painting has for me an ancient and elemental quality - which I associate with landscape, above all the landscape of Greece where I have spent some time in recent years.

The closely modulated variants of this colour are layered over one another to create an expansive veil of light, emanating from and through a central recessive space. A scheme of abstracted images progresses through this space, bound on either side by areas of linear tension.

The idea was to combine, in one work, opposing sensations of compression and release - tension and tranquillity.

John Bicknell was born in Surrey in 1958. He studied at West Surrey College of Art and Design 1975-77, North East London Polytechnic 1977-80 and the Slade School 1981-83. In 1983 he won a Slade Prize and a Boise Travelling Scholarship to Italy. His first one-man show was in 1987 at the Carlile Gallery London; in the same year he was a prizewinner in John Moores 15 and in the South Bank Picture Show, Royal Festival Hall London. In 1989-90 he was Henry Moore Printmaking Fellow at Leeds Polytechnic and he currently lectures there part-time. His most recent one-man exhibition was at Pomeroy Purdy Gallery London 1990.

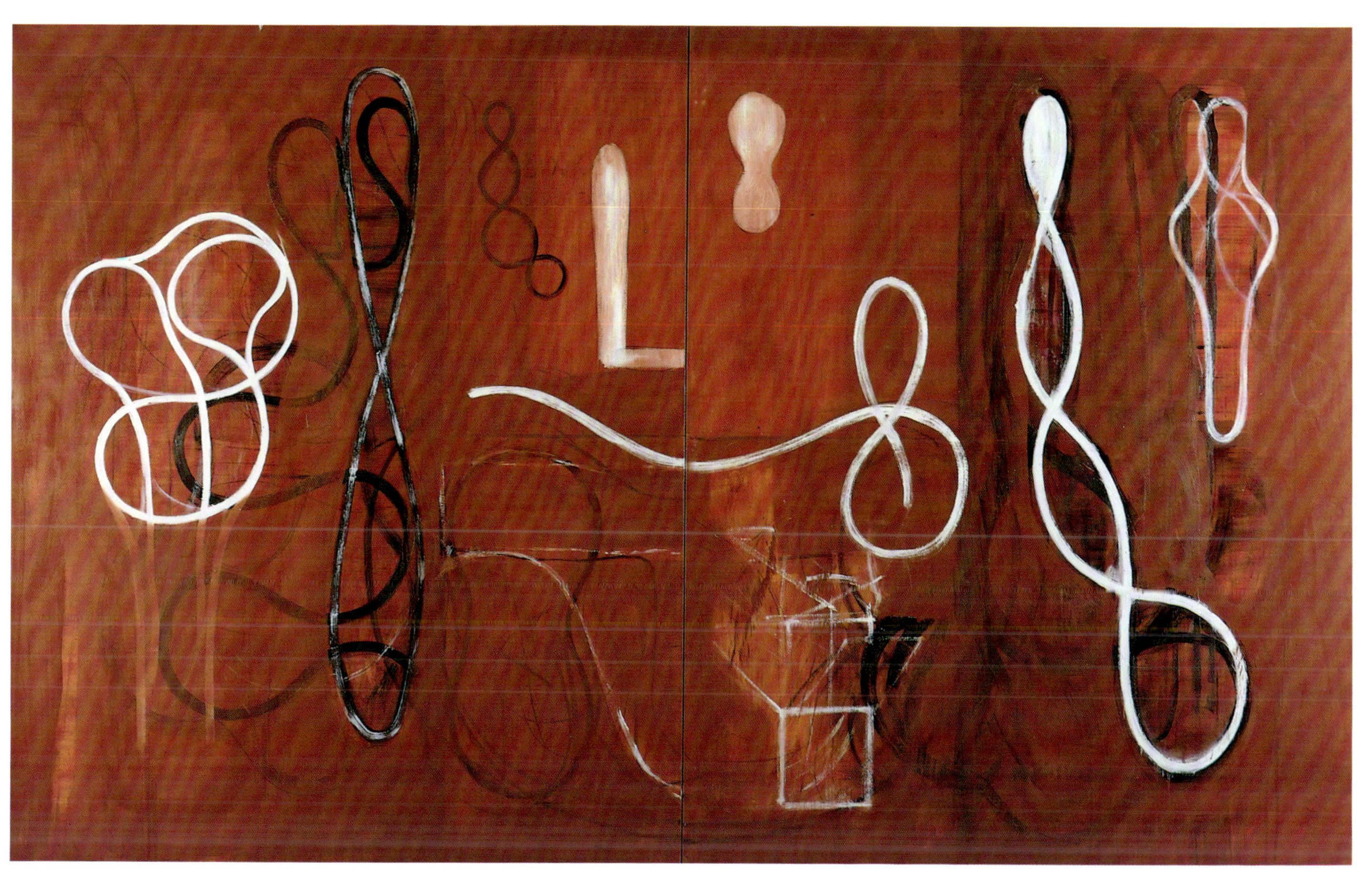

LICIA BRONZIN
WOMAN WITH COLOURS

oil on canvas   85.5 x 91.5 cm

Colours and Form, Shapes containing Colours
    The Colours in Nature are Innumerable
    They cannot be reproduced if not by an Emotion
    In our daily life we often dwell on the same things which return
                      to mind,
Colours that make Forms
Forms that make Features - a Nose
                 - a Mouth
                 - Eyes
They become my Obsession for Life

Everyday I see Obsession - Not for Love
                 - for Beauty
                 - for Desire
                  - for Liberty
                 - To Choose Life
            Obsession for Possession
            Obsession for Power
                 - Carefully Avoiding Death

Licia Bronzin was born in 1960 in Adelaide, Australia. She studied painting at the Academy of Fine Arts, Venice 1980-84 and Film and Video at the London College of Printing 1987-90. She exhibited at the New Era Gallery, Adelaide in 1985 but this is her first major British show. She is currently working on a film combining live action and animation, and on a series of portraits.

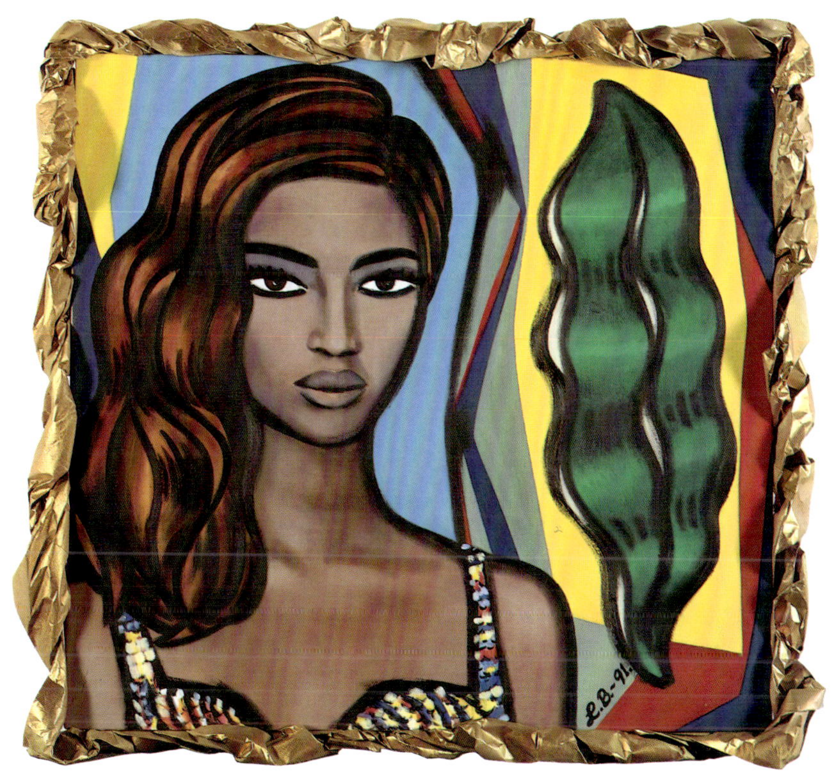

L.B.-91

GRAHAM CHORLTON
APARTMENT

acrylic on canvas   149 x 179.5 cm

..."Yet these paintings comply neither with a notion of realism attached to the on-the-spot empiricism of the Impressionists, nor with the formalist conception of the 'realism' of the autonomous art object. They seek a psychological reality which takes account of historical representations of the urban experience ceaselessly re-invented in the media and the arts".

(Robert Burstow, in the catalogue *Unfinished Business,* Lanchester Gallery 1990)

Graham Chorlton was born in Leicester in 1953. He studied at the University of Leeds 1972-76 and at Birmingham Polytechnic 1977-78. Since 1978 his one-man shows include Wolverhampton Art Gallery 1983 and Midlands Arts Centre 1989; recent group shows include *Facade: The City's Face,* Ikon Gallery Birmingham and tour 1987-88; *Inter City 88,* Birmingham and Sheffield 1988 and *Unfinished Business,* Lanchester Gallery, Coventry Polytechnic 1990. Commissions include works painted for Birmingham City Council and Visitor and Convention Bureau. He currently lectures part-time at Birmingham Polytechnic and two further West Midlands colleges.

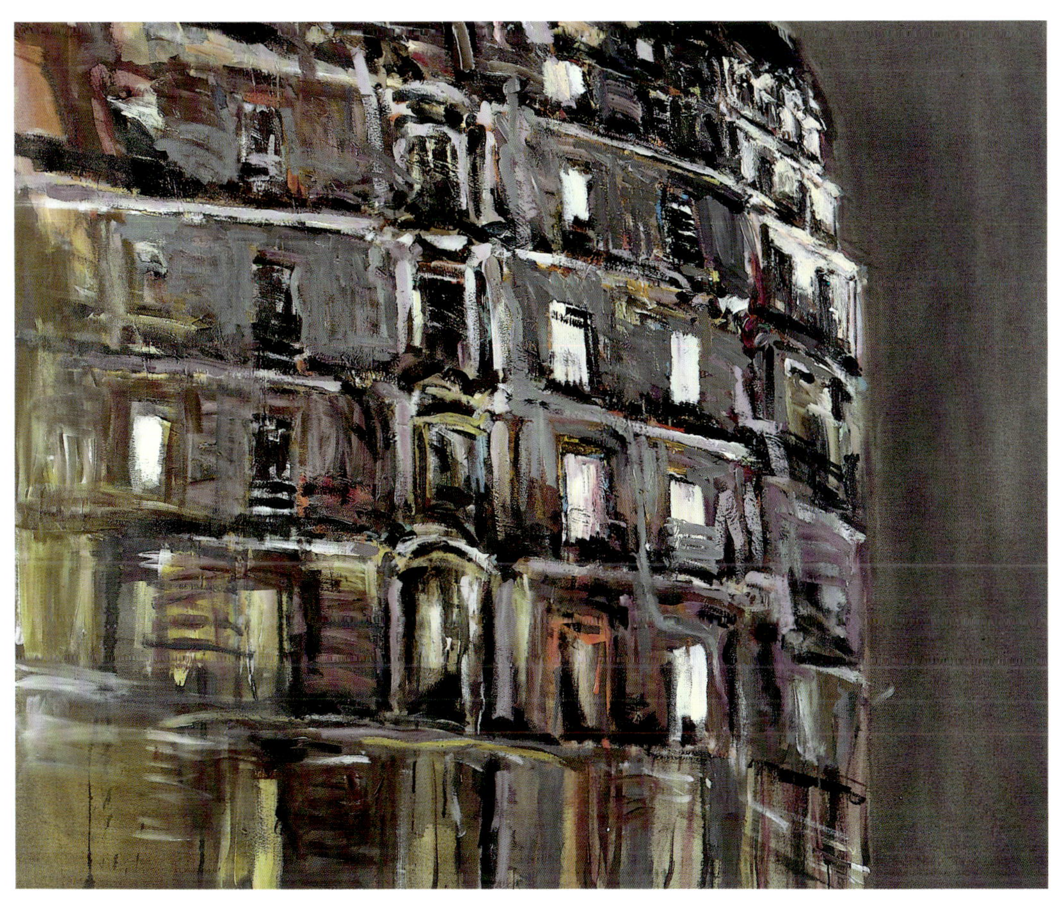

RUPERT CLAUSEN
PASSING THROUGH

oil on canvas 157 x 200cm

Passing Through depicts biomorphic forms in an abstracted drama.

Rupert Clausen was born in Copenhagen in 1960. He studied at South Glamorgan Institute of Higher Education 1978-79 and Birmingham Polytechnic 1979-82. He showed in John Moores 16, 1989. He will be represented in *The Discerning Eye*, Mall Galleries London in late '91 and a one-man show at York University is projected for May 1992.

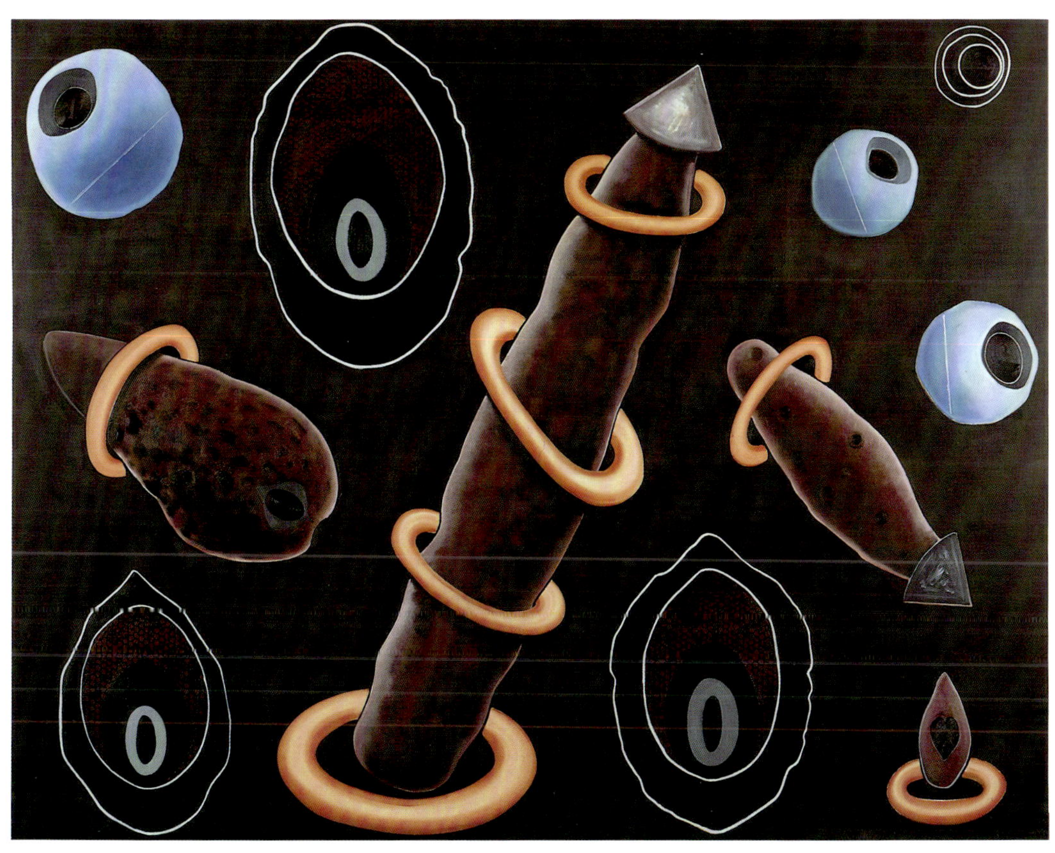

PETER CLOSSICK
THE RANGER'S HOUSE

oil on canvas   153 x 183.5 cm

The Ranger's House is partly about childhood experience - I often used to play the Lone Ranger as a child.

I think when you paint, when you project something, you know inside yourself whether you are being truthful or doing a cover-up job. That is, given your understanding of truth at that particular moment in time.

The house is a seventeenth-century building in Greenwich Park. As a view, set in the park across Blackheath, I pass it frequently. In my urge to paint a landscape I became engrossed in it as a motif. I feel pleased if people find the results worth looking at. It is a record of my journey.

Peter Clossick was born in London in 1948. He studied at Leicester Polytechnic 1966-69, Camberwell School of Art 1974-78 and Goldsmiths' College 1978-79. He has been included regularly in shows in London since 1984, including the London Group, Spirit of London, R.O.I., Whitechapel Open, and R.A. Summer Show. In 1989 he had a one-man show at the Sweet Waters Gallery London and recently has had shows at the Woodlands Art Gallery, Bow House Gallery Hertfordshire and Phoenix Gallery, Highgate (October '91). He is a full time art lecturer in Adult Education.

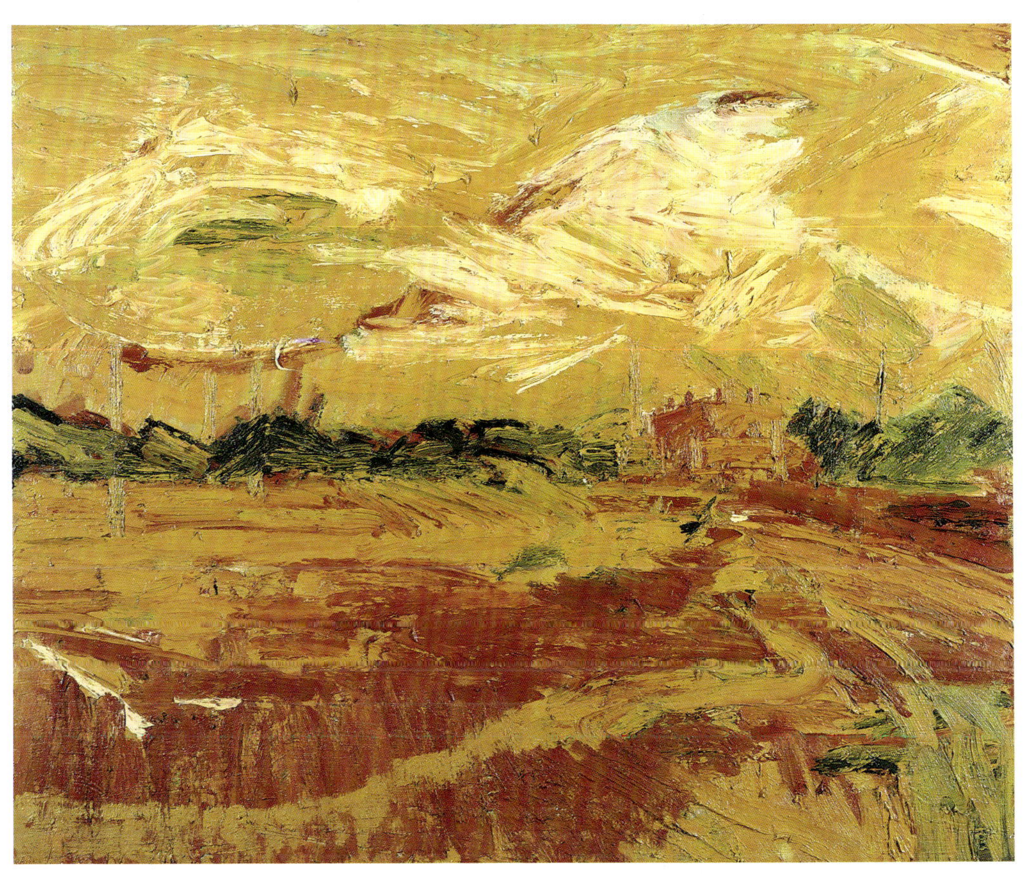

BRENDAN COLVERT
UNTITLED

oil and black tar varnish   220.5 x 165.5cm
on canvas

The Problem of Pain

A demonic figure of ill-omen scatters the seeds
of destruction.

**Brendan Colvert was born in Dorset in 1961. He
studied at Bristol Polytechnic 1984-87. His work has
been seen in a mixed show at Northlands,
Cheltenham; the Bristol/Hanover Exhibition, Bristol,
both 1987; and in collaborations at The Cottages,
Bristol 1989 and the St Johns Road Site Bristol 1989.**

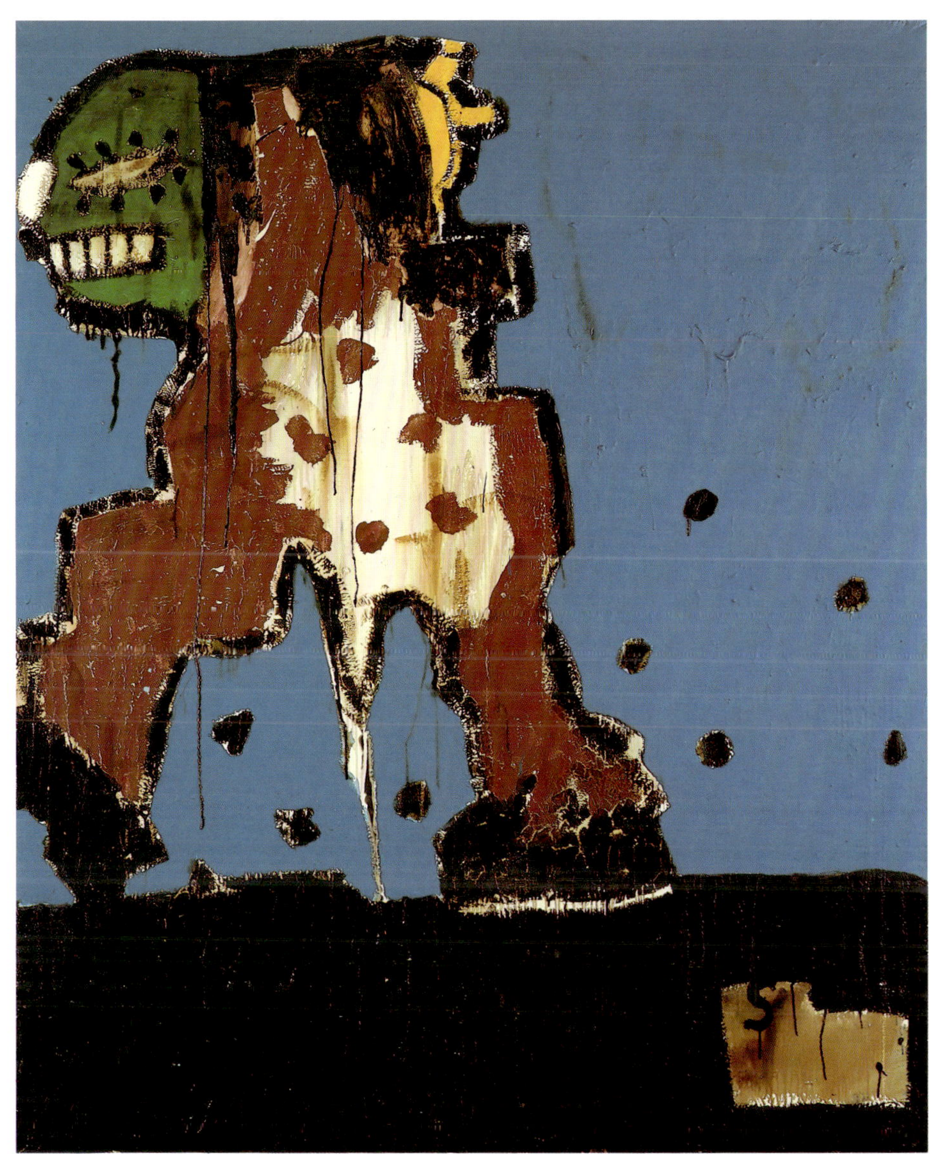

TERRY DUFFY
THE MIRACULOUS DRAUGHT OF FISHES

oil on canvas   275 x 254cm

.... Many things can be described in detail but the deeper, richer and more intangible they are the more difficult it becomes ....

Terry Duffy was born in Liverpool in 1948 and studied at Liverpool College of Art 1973-76. His one-man shows include Air Gallery London 1981, Harris Museum (North-West Arts Major Fellowship) 1984, Blom and Dorn New York 1985 and the Laing Art Gallery, Newcastle-upon-Tyne 1989. In 1991 he has shown in the Hunting Award exhibition and his work has been seen in London at the CAS art market and the Francis Graham-Dixon, Benjamin Rhodes and Gillian Jason Galleries. He is Liverpool Chairman of the British Art and Design Association.

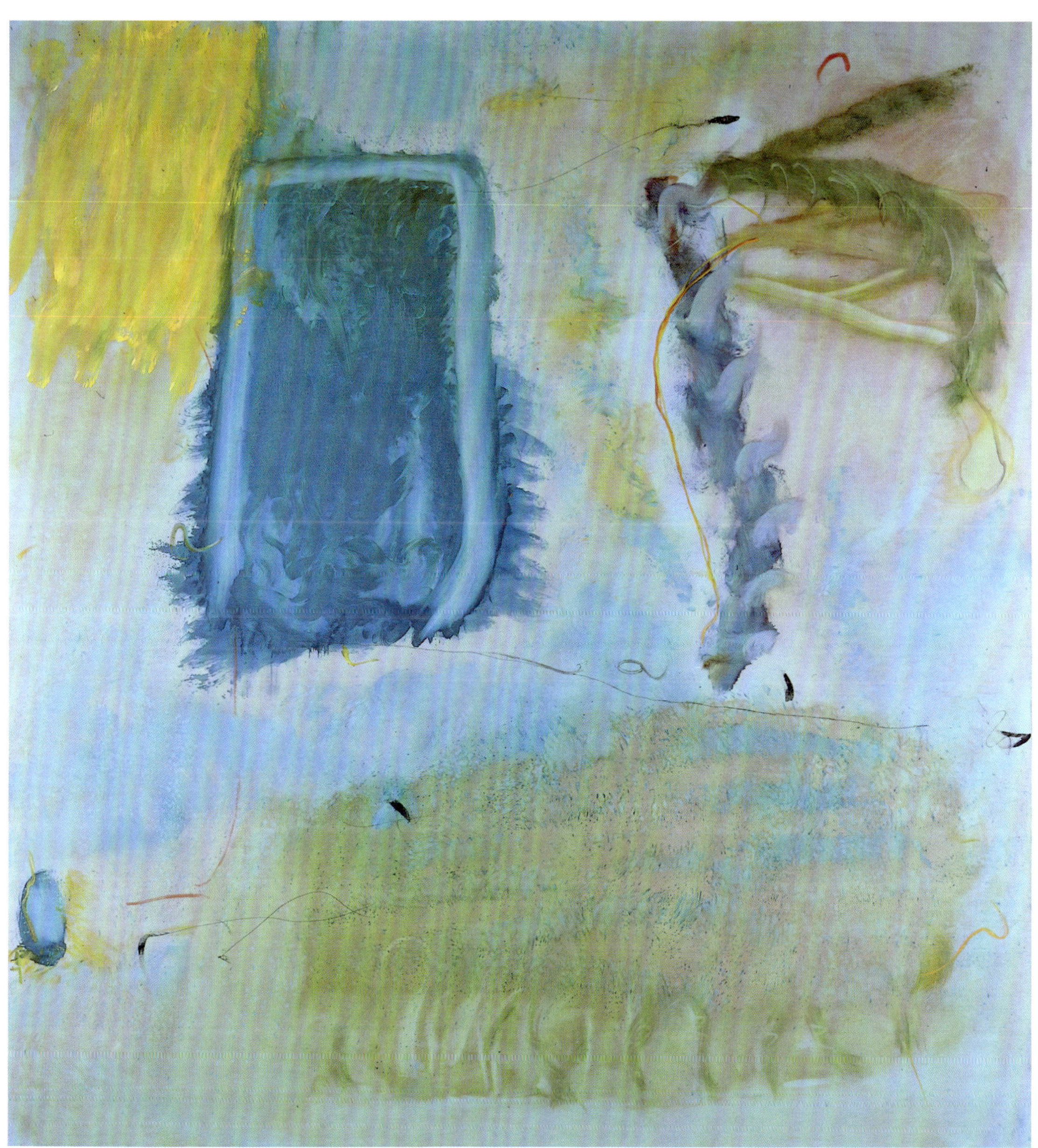

TRICIA GILLMAN
BUSY BEE

oil on canvas   122 x 122.5 cm

Busy Bee belongs to a group of paintings which essentially allow no resting place for the eye; all are very active, highly wrought and intensely coloured. The vocabulary of shape derives clearly from plant form and cycles of growth. Shape relations are impacted, tightly juxtaposed, over-layered, revealed and eclipsed. The square format restrains and equalises potentially explosive internal energies. I hope the painting speaks of a process of regeneration through its manipulation of speed, excess and dichotomy encountered en route to a sought equilibrium.

Tricia Gillman was born in Johannesburg in 1951. She studied at the Universities of Leeds 1970-74 and Newcastle-upon-Tyne 1975-77. Her first one-woman show was held at the Parkinson Gallery Leeds in 1978, and subsequent solo shows have included Arnolfini Bristol 1985, Benjamin Rhodes Gallery London 1985, '87 and '89 and Laing Art Gallery Newcastle (touring) 1989-90. She was included in *Forces of Nature,* Manchester City Art Gallery 1990 and *Three Ways,* British Council touring to Eastern Europe 1990. This is her fourth John Moores since first appearing in 1982.

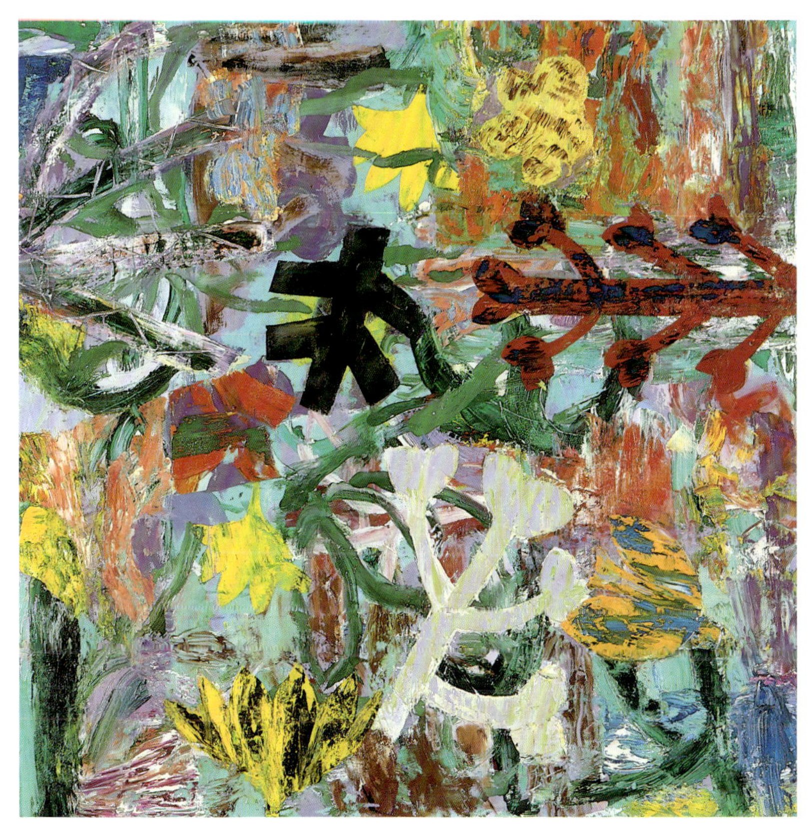

LAURA GODFREY-ISAACS
BODY WITH LITTLE WHITE HOLES

oil on canvas   188.5 x 200cm

Seeing the painting as 'body,' the surfaces become personal and suggestive and images emerge from a highly-charged skin sculpted out of paint. Small white circles, which could be eyes, are built up in paint to form deep holes; they proliferate the surface and edges of the painting, rendering the 'body' fragile and vulnerable.

Comedy and tragedy mix as these little holes peep out of the surface and the position of the painting becomes uncertain, shifting uneasily between provocative physicality and sensual allure.

Laura Godfrey-Isaacs was born in London 1964. She studied at Kingston Polytechnic 1982, Brighton Polytechnic 1983-86 and the Slade School 1986-88. In 1988 she won a Boise award and a Fulbright Fellowship to be Artist-in-Residence at the Pratt Institute in Brooklyn, New York and in 1990 she was Artist-in-Residence at the Tate Gallery Liverpool. This concluded with her solo show *Pink*. Other one-woman shows have been at Monima Gallery London and Morgan's Gallery London, both 1989, and Sue Williams Gallery and John Milton Gallery London, 1991.

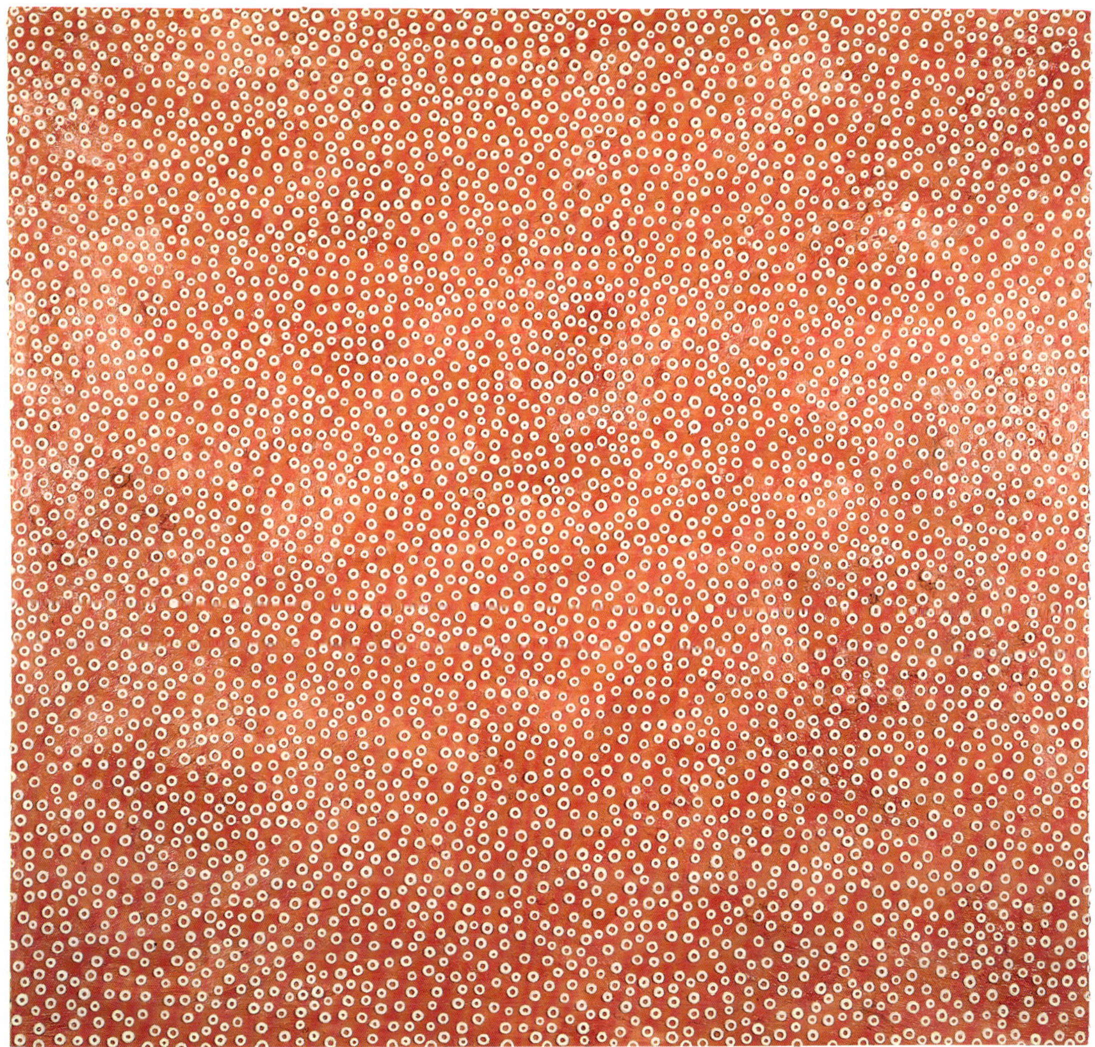

MARTIN GREENLAND
THE MINOTAUR'S PALACE

oil on canvas   79.5 x 129.5 cm

Real situations or circumstances can have a massive power that enables the mind naturally to open up and develop them in terms of paint and imagery.

Here the situation is essentially the same as in *Rich* (John Moores 16) but the theme is expanded.

This is wasteland which is raw, basic and natural. In its natural state it reveals delicacy, strength, autonomy, co-existence and majestic interdependence. Some of these qualities one finds in the Minotaurs of Picasso's *Vollard Suite.* I had already used the figure of the bull to convey concentrated ideas of simmering power, tenderness and dignity; in the Minotaur, a mythological figure which I felt I was using with a purposeful object, I hoped to carry these qualities from bull to man. I wanted to give both it and the woman individual, independent strength but create a strong sexual bond between them.

Martin Greenland was born in Marsden, West Yorkshire, in 1962. He studied at Exeter College of Art 1982-85. His exhibitions include the Whitworth Young Contemporaries 1985, Gallery North, Kirkby Lonsdale 1987 and '88, and John Moores 16 1989. He is based in Kendal and a permanent display of his work may be seen there at the New Year Gallery which adjoins his studio.

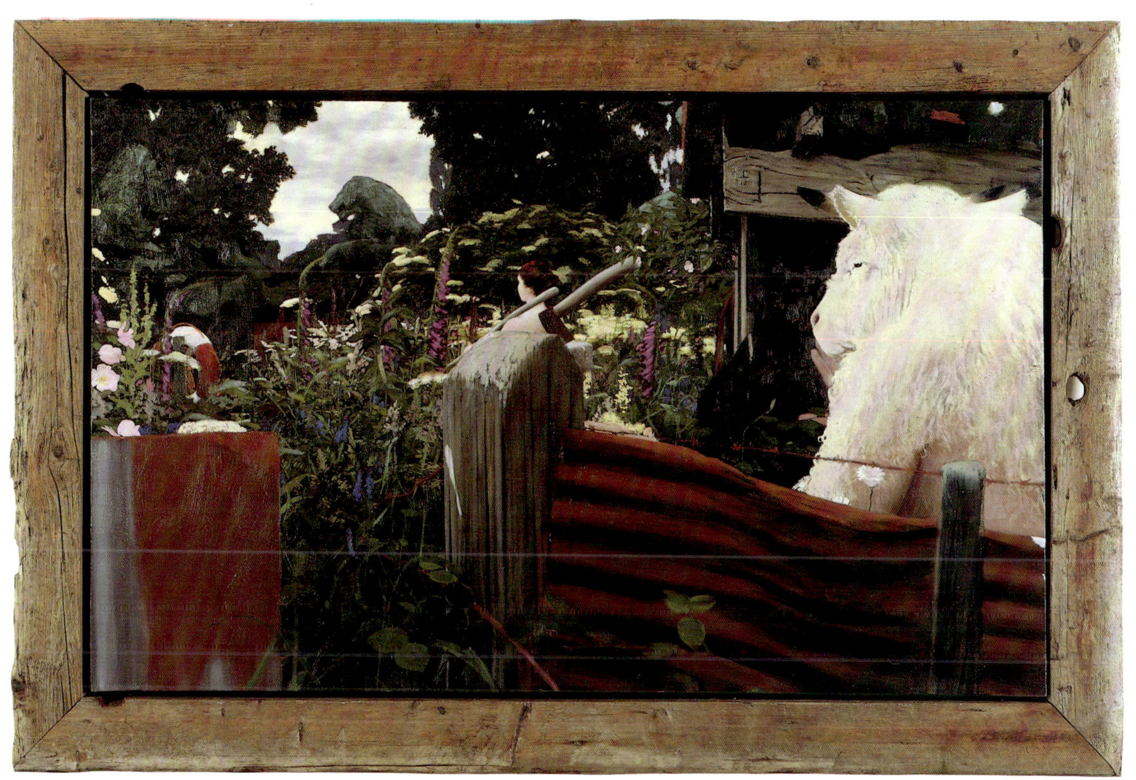

TREVOR HALLIDAY
THE VALE OF VIRTUE AND VICE

oil on canvas   127.5 x 152.5 cm

This is a medium-scale allegorical painting in a series of works that are forming a bridge between my mythological subjects (based on a theme of 'the mythological figure in the landscape') and projects I have in mind for the future.

It was completed this year employing a technique of high definition which describes the form with weight and ponderosity.

The title describes the landscape that the hermaphroditic figure finds on this place of earthly mortality.

As a visual rather than a literary artist I hope the painting will reveal its meaning if the viewer has the patience.

Trevor Halliday was born in Birmingham in 1939. He studied at Birmingham College of Arts and Crafts 1954-60 and at the Royal Academy Schools 1960-63. His major exhibitions include *Objects and Documents* (Arts Council 1971-72), *Recent British Painting,* Hayward Gallery 1974, a one-man retrospective at the IKON Gallery Birmingham 1975; University Gallery Nottingham 1979; *Twenty One for Twenty One* IKON Gallery and Hong Kong 1985. He has lectured widely in Fine Art Departments nationally and until 1989 was Head of the Fine Art School, Birmingham Polytechnic. Between 1987 and 1989 he completed a CNAA award MPhil in Fine Art when his concluding show was *The Mythological Figure in the Landscape* (Birmingham 1989).

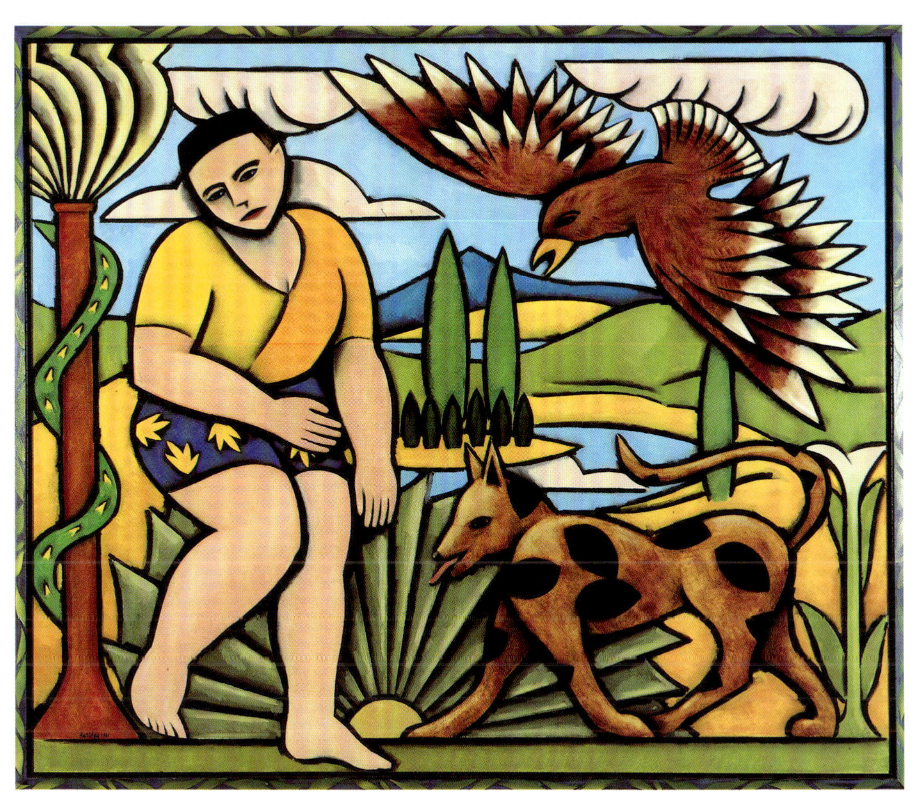

PAUL HAMLYN
LUCIFER

oil on canvas   221.5 x 259cm

This painting portrays a cycle of mischief whereby the impossibility of pure perception, expression and contact traps the characters in a cheerfully brutal cartoon existence.

Paul Hamlyn was born in Stockport in 1953. He studied at Goldsmiths' College 1979-80 and St Martin's School of Art 1980-83, returning to Goldsmiths' 1986-88. In 1991 he created the site-specific mixed media installation PITCH and exhibited at Alternative Arts, both in London.

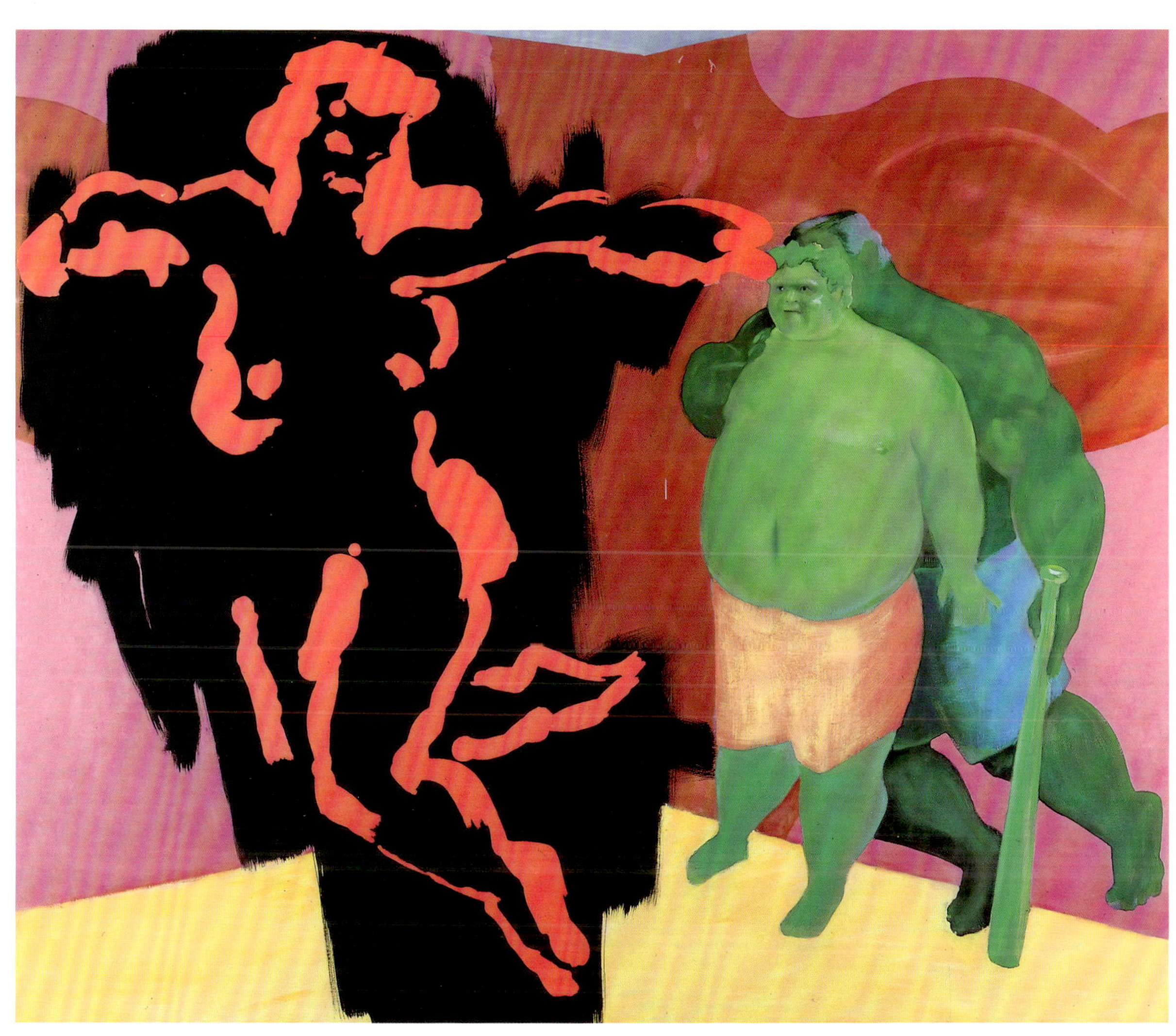

JOEL HAMMOND
THREE

acrylic on canvas   182.5 x 106.5 cm

The three people in this painting are: myself in the middle, my father at the bottom and a stranger at the top. The place is a cinema; the film is about the loss of a friend.

The colours are a reflection of the screen. Time spent on the painting: eighteen hours.

Joel Hammond was born in Littletown, Co. Durham in 1963. He is self-taught as an artist and this is his first major exhibition.

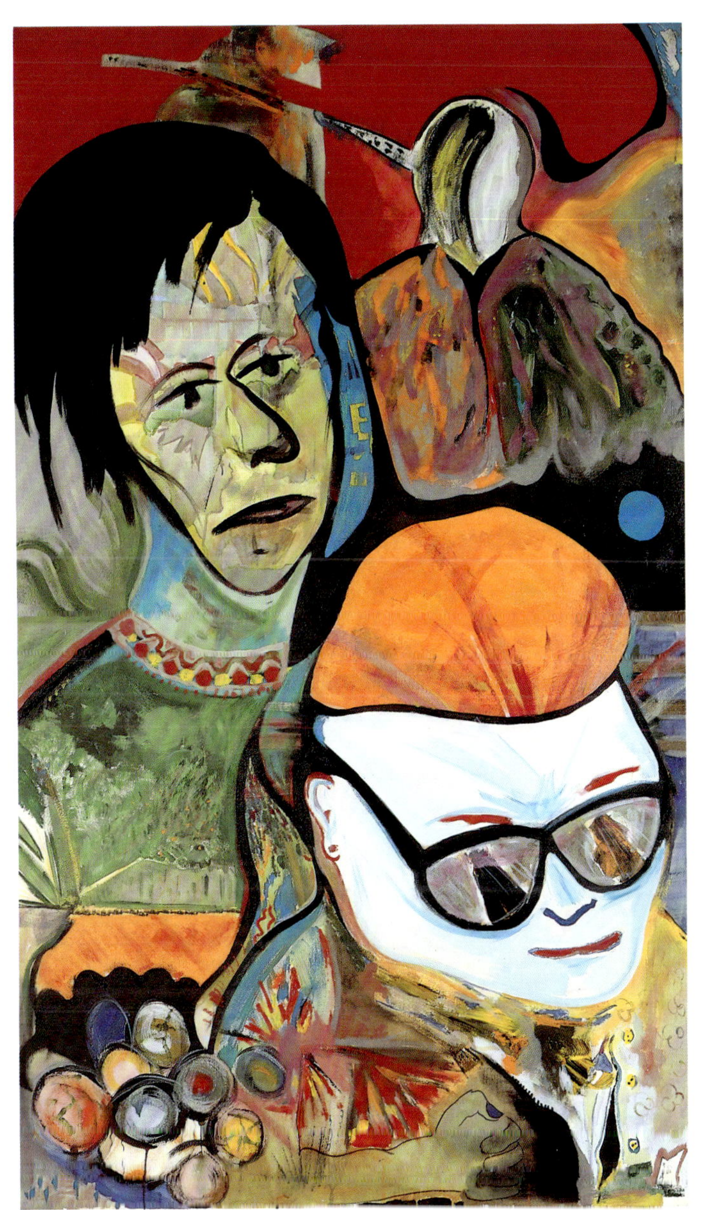

PAUL HOUSLEY
THE ELECTRICIAN

oil on canvas   148 x 127.5 cm

The Electrician, also known as *John Garfield,* came into existence after I had destroyed a number of bad paintings which I had come to regard as the daubings of a rank amateur.

The right hand had chastised the left and out of bad came good. How sad the painter who thinks he has found the way to paint.

Paul Housley was born in Stalybridge in 1964. He studied at Tameside College of Technology 1981-82 and Sheffield Polytechnic 1983-86. He has exhibited in London at Smith's Gallery and the Islington Arts Factory and in Sheffield in group shows at the Graves and Mappin Art Galleries.

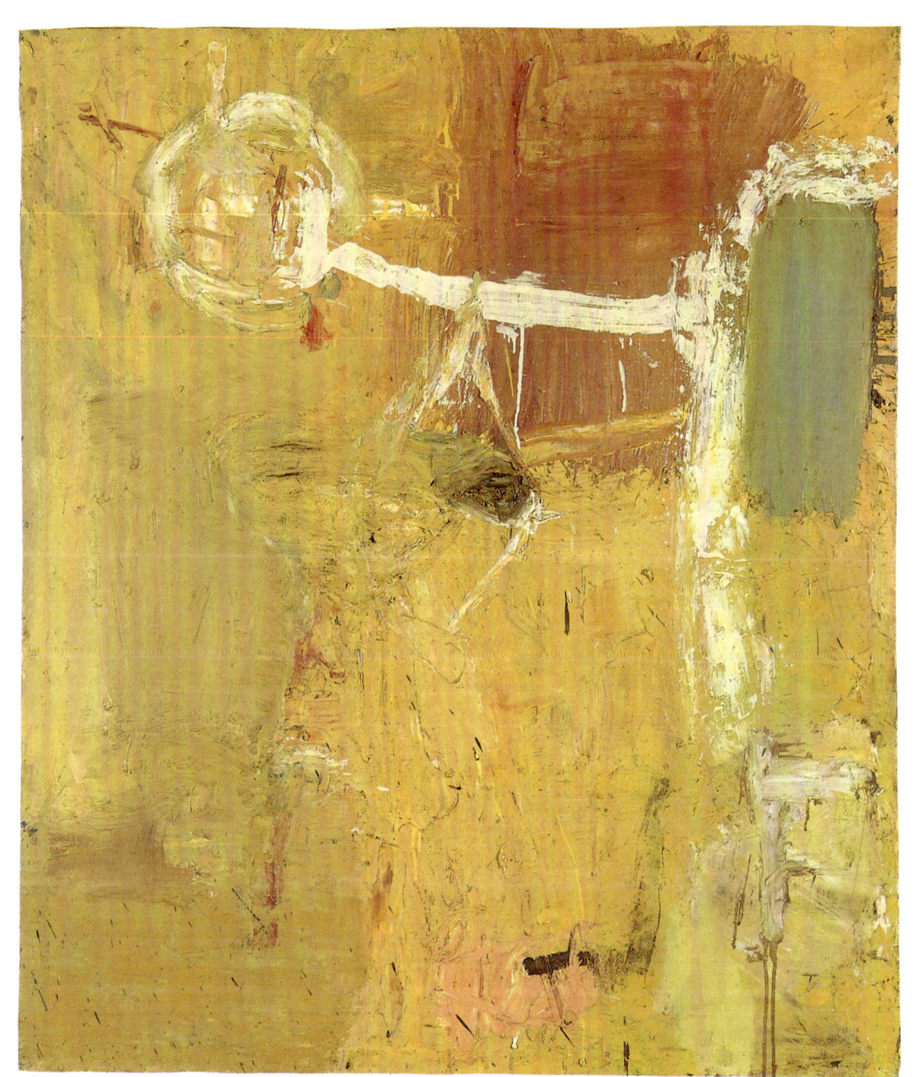

JOHN HUBBARD
COURTYARD STILL LIFE

oil on canvas   172.5 x 183 cm

This painting dates from about midway through my exploration of the theme of the courtyard garden, which began in 1987. The immediate source is one of the courtyards in the Alhambra, which I have visited many times and where I have made numerous black and white studies. My interest is the intermingling of interior and exterior space and of the man-made with the 'natural'. This offers almost endless possibilities of making palpable the spiritual and physical 'reality' of the place without resorting to banal description. Each subject, however, contains its own individual characteristics. *Courtyard Still Life* also has oblique references to some of Matisse's still lives made before the First World War. Art is full of such connections.

John Hubbard was born in 1931 at Ridgefield, Connecticut, USA. He studied at Harvard University 1950-53 and from 1956 to 1958 in New York and Provincetown. He moved to England and his first one-man exhibition was at the New Art Centre London 1961. Since then he has had many one-man and group shows in Britain and internationally. Since his 1986 retrospective at the Yale Center for British Art, New Haven his major exhibitions have included one-man shows at the Armstrong Gallery New York 1987 and Fischer Fine Art London 1988 and 1991 (forthcoming); in 1988 his residency at New Harmony, Indiana resulted in the New Harmony Project (seen at the Curwen Gallery London 1990); in 1990 he spent time as guest artist at the National Gallery of Malaysia (*Images of Malaysia*, Malaysian tour 1990) and won the Astra Award to paint a courtyard garden for West Dorset Hospital.

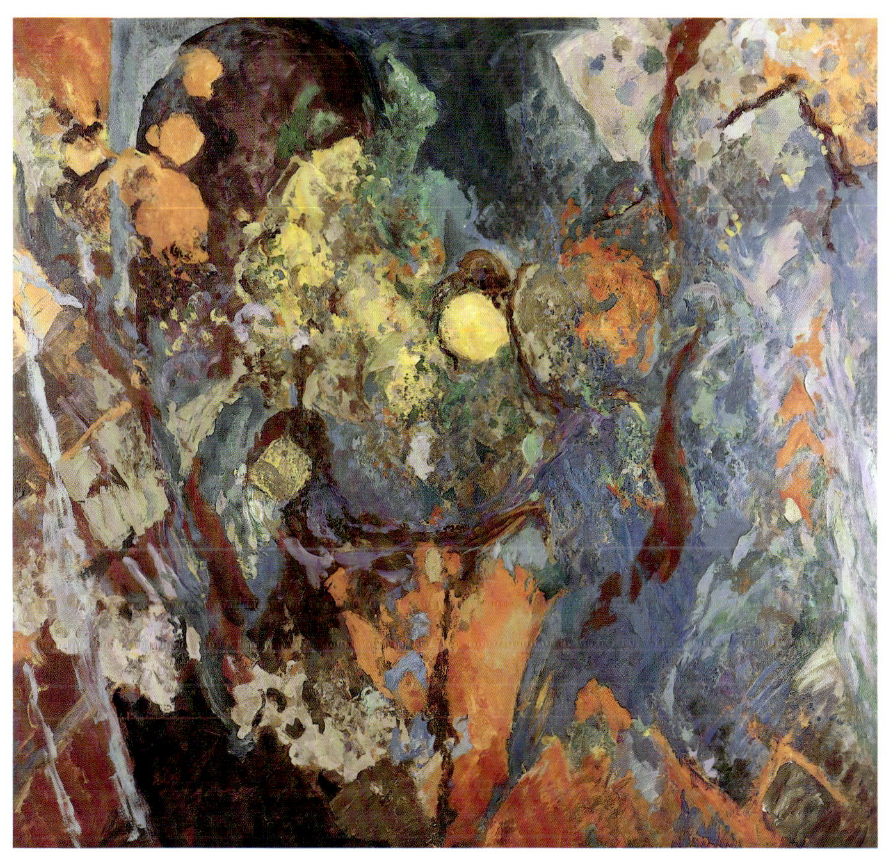

DAVID INSHAW
PORTRAIT OF SILBURY HILL: MAY 1989

oil on canvas   127 x 145cm

I lived near Silbury Hill for nearly twenty years and painted it many times.

It is the most spectacular of all the prehistoric monuments in Wiltshire and it presents a mystery: why was it built, what meaning did it have for the people who built it and what does it mean to us today? To some, the mystery is enough; to others it gives an insight into pre-historic philosophy which could have relevance for us today. I have passed the hill many times on my way home and have experienced it in all its aspects. While the shape remains constant, the appearance is ever-changing with the time of day or season of the year. It seems to convey, in a very dramatic way and in a way no natural structure could, all the problems of reconciling the moment with a larger grasp of time. Its extraordinary presence acts as a timeless focus for our efforts to understand our environment.

I painted this picture as it was when I left Wiltshire.

David Inshaw was born in Wednesfield, Staffs, in 1943. He studied at Beckenham School of Art 1959-63 and the Royal Academy Schools 1963-66. His first one-man show was at the Arnolfini Gallery Bristol 1969. In the mid-1970s he was a member of the Ruralists Group with whom he exhibited regularly over the next decade, and from 1975 to 1977 he held a Fellowship in Creative Art at Trinity College Cambridge. Subsequent one-man exhibitions have taken place at Brighton Pavilion Gallery 1978, Waddington Galleries London 1980, '84 and '89 and Nishimura Gallery Tokyo 1987.

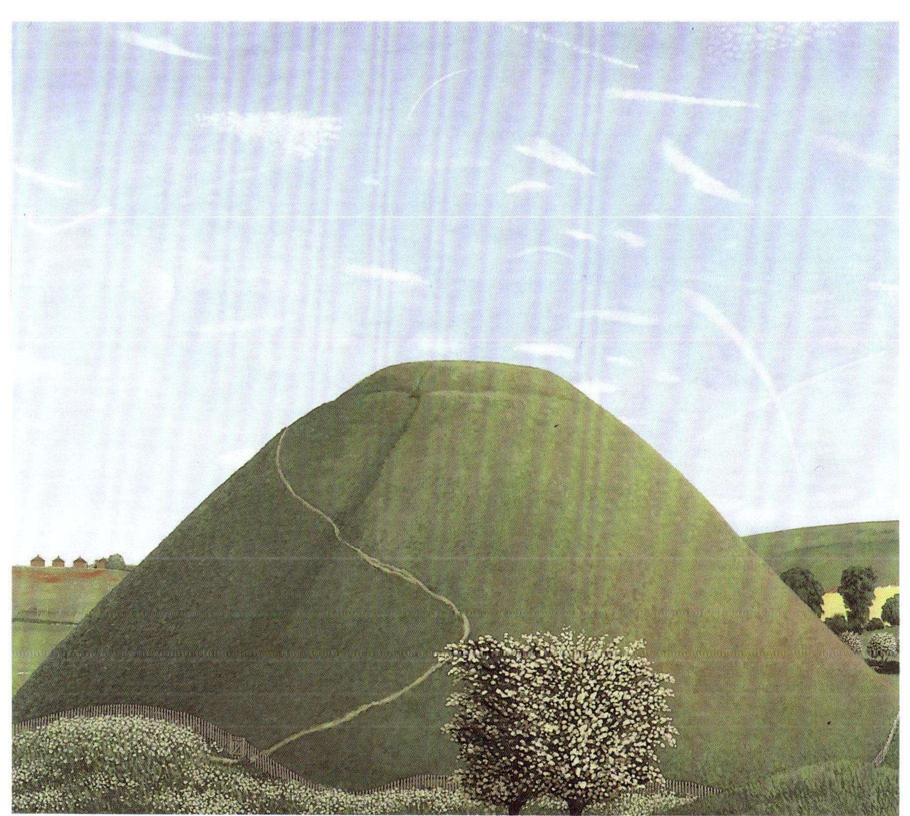

ALBERT IRVIN
SKIPPER

acrylic on canvas   214 x 306cm

'Skipper' is the name of a street in Belfast opposite Benny's A1 bar, where the Guinness is bliss and I have enjoyed memorable meetings with friends.

The painting may be seen as a homage to Benny and my Belfast friends and their beautiful, hospitable, poignant city.

Albert Irvin was born in London 1922. He studied at Northampton School of Art 1940-41 and Goldsmiths' College 1946-50. His first one-man shows were at 57 Gallery Edinburgh 1960 and the New Art Centre London 1961, where he exhibited regularly throughout the '60s and '70s. He taught at Goldsmiths' College 1962-83. Since then he has exhibited widely in this country and abroad. His most recent one-man exhibition was at the Serpentine Gallery and tour 1990, and major recent group shows include *The Great British Art Show* Glasgow 1990 and the Goldsmiths' Centenary 1990. In 1992 he will have one-man shows at Gimpel Fils London and in Frankfurt and Valencia. This is his sixth appearance in the John Moores.

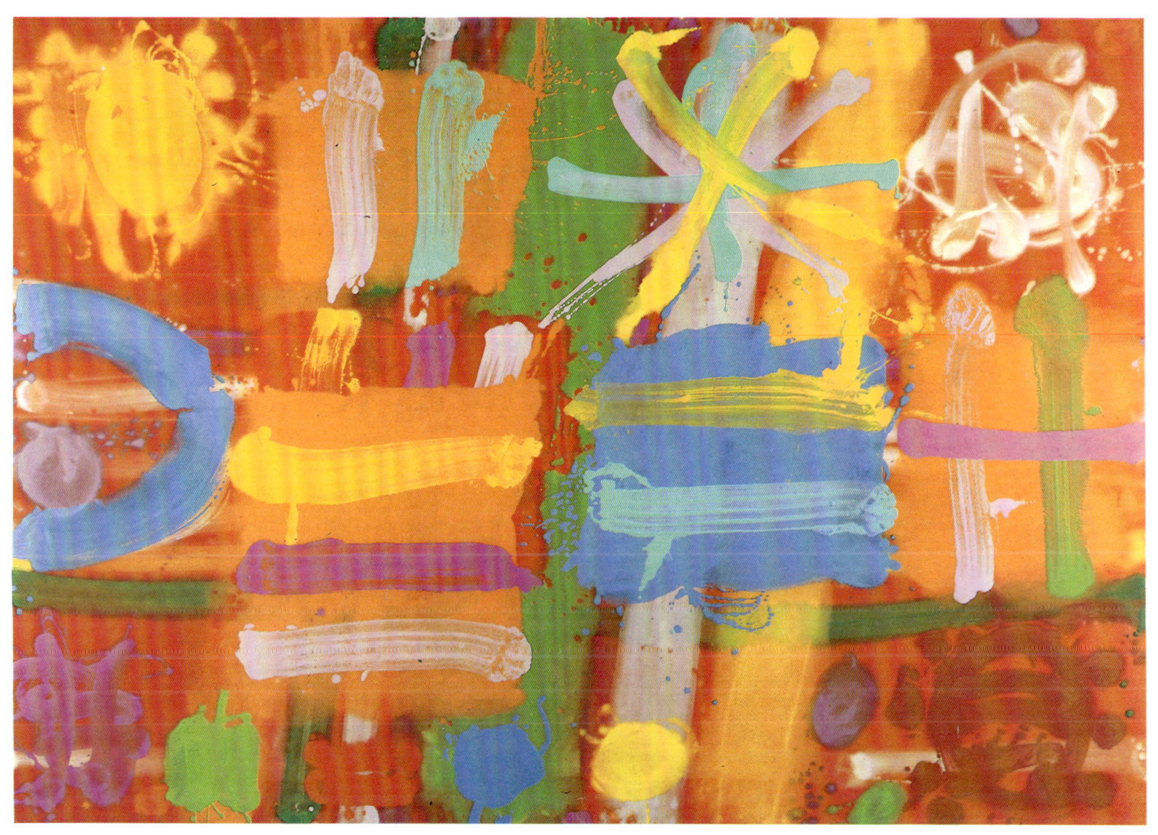

RICHARD KEMP
BIG SUR

mixed media on canvas   202.5 x 172.5 cm

Big Sur is painted in stages, or layers. Each layer establishes a position in space which subsequent layers contradict. The final layer of the painting stands proud of the surface yet reads pictorially as receding. The painting can be read both as a picture and as a progression outward into the world.

I have introduced concrete space into my recent work not to subvert a genre but in order to gain greater clarity. There is a common misconception that abstract painting is either about universal generalisations or about pure formalism (whatever that is). My painting is abstract because I want to create specific metaphors. It is a painting about very simple sentiments. The very simple sentiment behind this painting is Birth (the wonder of). It is specifically about the birth of my son, George. It is a metaphor for coming into being.

Richard Kemp was born in Croydon, Surrey in 1958. He studied at Croydon College of Art and Design 1974-76 and Ravensbourne College of Art and Design 1977-80. He held his first one-man show at the Greenwich Theatre Art Gallery in 1984 and group shows since 1979 include *New Contemporaries,* ICA 1979, *Northern Young Contemporaries,* Whitworth Art Gallery Manchester 1979, *Pacesetters II,* Peterborough Museum 1982; London Group 1985, Carpenters Road Open Studios 1988, '89, '91 and group shows at Pomeroy Purdy Gallery 1989 and '91.

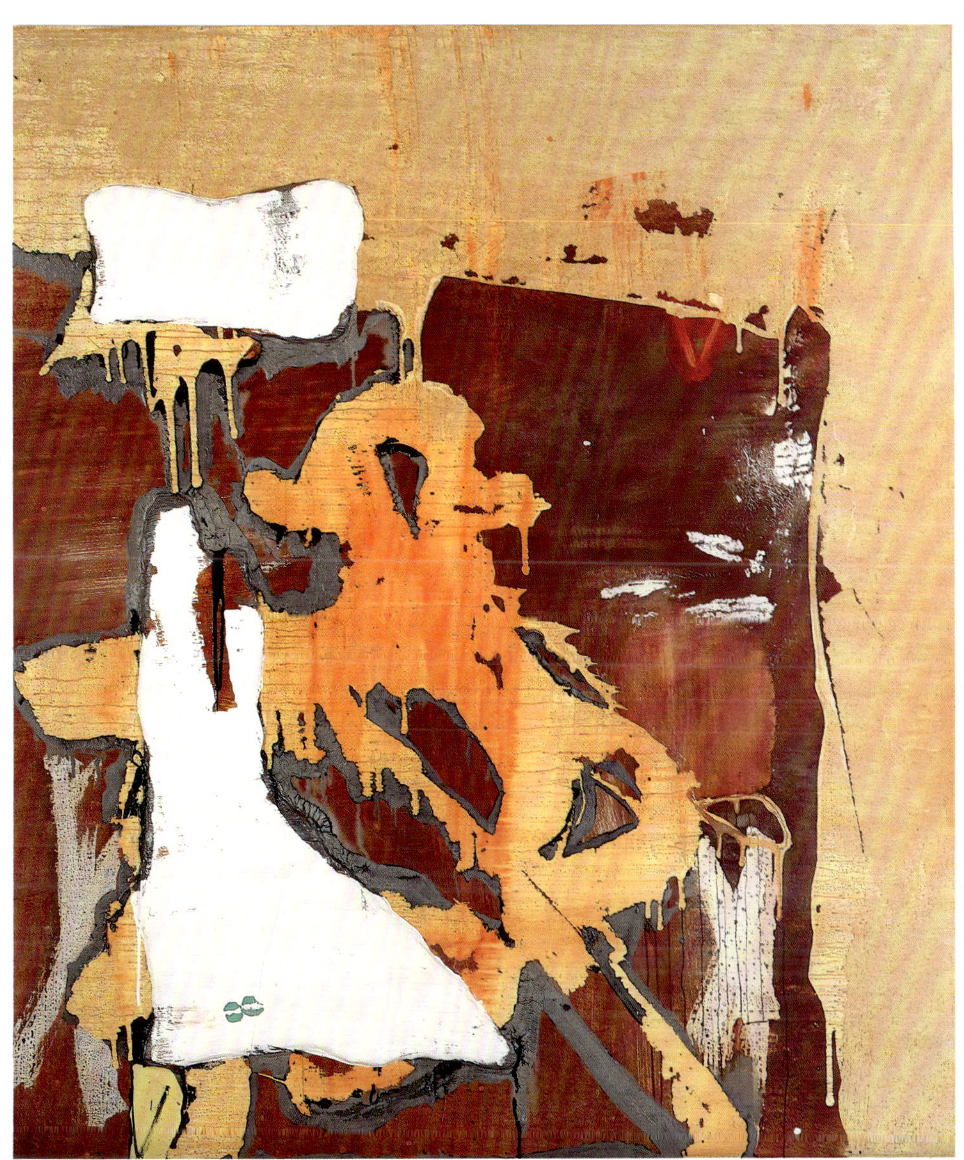

KHAN
VIRGIN OF THE RADIATOR

acrylic on metal   47 x 55 cm

I work with mixed media and do not restrict myself in ideas. Recently I have been using junk from scrap yards; either painting on it or incorporating it within paintings. In this case I had found two radiators, the smaller of which seemed like a baby. The idea of a mother and child was triggered off. I looked at the Virgin and Child paintings at the National Gallery, incorporating features from different paintings as the form of the found object required, but especially from the Madonna of the Basket by Correggio. Hence the title for my own work.

Khan was born in Ranpur, India in 1952. He trained as an engineer before beginning art studies at the Camden Arts Centre in 1976. After appearing in an exhibition there in 1978 he continued his studies at Middlesex Polytechnic 1978-79 and North-East London Polytechnic 1979-82. This is his first major subsequent exhibition.

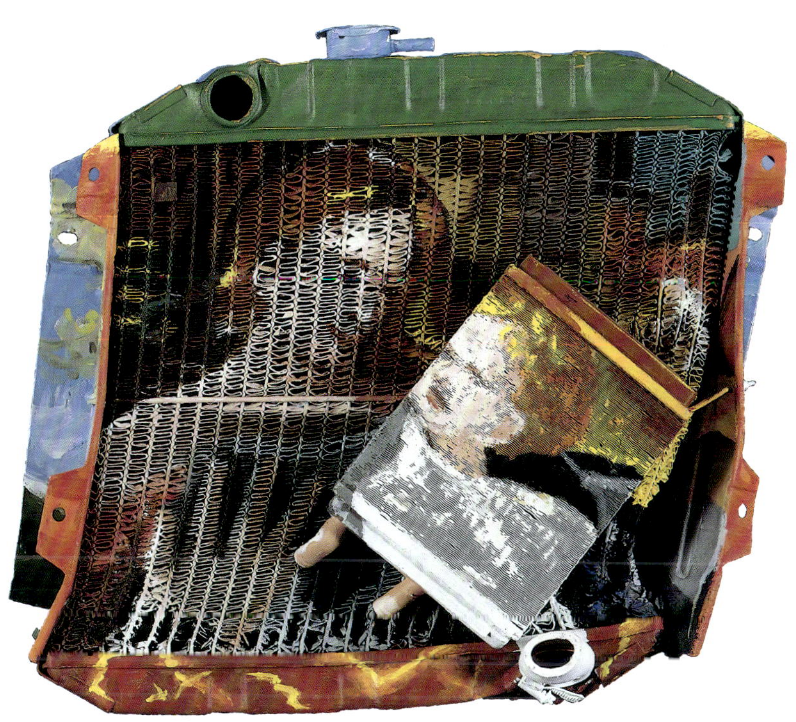

MIKE KNOWLES
MYNYDD EILIAN, WINDY DAY, SUMMER

oil on canvas   112 x 122 cm

This painting is one of a continuing series of the countryside surrounding our home in Anglesey. It is a portrait of a hedge with the hillside of Mynydd Eilian in the distance. It was begun hesitantly - worked on outdoors over many sessions and completely reworked in one hectic, perhaps desperate, afternoon. A particular light and a freshening wind helped to establish the rhythms and space of the image.

In the past I have been concerned most often with panoramic views, drawn to horizons and the western sky, and it has taken me some years to be able to grasp the possibilities of a more intimate scale. In this and many other ways my vision of the world has been influenced by my wife's startlingly unpretentious paintings and their attention to the complexity of facts. Monet's dictum "observation and reflection" seems ever more relevant.

Mike Knowles was born in Warrington in 1941. He studied at Liverpool College of Art 1959-63 and at the Slade School 1964-66, where he won the Tonks Drawing Prize and Landscape Painting Prize. His first one-man show was at the Bluecoat Gallery Liverpool 1967 since when he has shown regularly in London, North Wales and the North-West, notably in *The Native Land: Welsh Landscape Painting since 1699*, Llandudno 1979, *The Probity of Art,* Welsh Arts Council 1979-80, and Riverside Studios 1982. He taught at Liverpool Polytechnic from 1967, as Head of Painting from 1983, until 1991 when he was elected Professor Emeritus in Fine Art. The Mostyn Art Gallery Llandudno will hold a retrospective of his work in 1992.

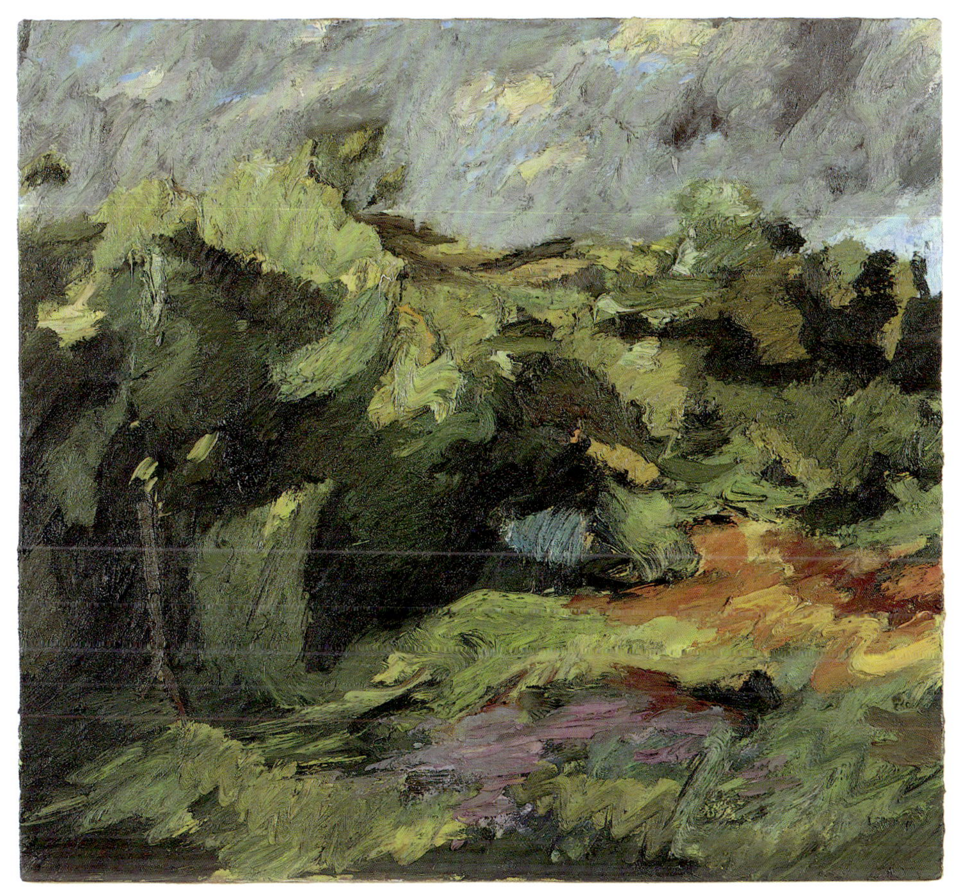

DIRK LARSEN
FRIDAY 7 P.M.

oil on card   63.5 x 84cm

I have formalised my thoughts into producing pictures so as to construct physical units of exchange. With these units (pictures) I aim to build a social context for my children to react to.

When I die my relatives will be left with a chess-game in mid flow: of pictures sold, lent, borrowed and stolen, which will continue so long as I have been rigorous enough in my endeavours.

Dirk Larsen was born in Copenhagen in 1951. He studied at Birmingham College of Art 1969-72 and the Royal College of Art 1972-75. In the mid 1980s he taught Alternative Studies at South Glamorgan Institute for Higher Education. His shows include *Documenta 6*, Kassel, and one-man shows in Amsterdam, New York, Cologne and two at the Produzentengalerie, Hamburg. He is currently making a sculptural piece for Stuttgart Garden Festival.

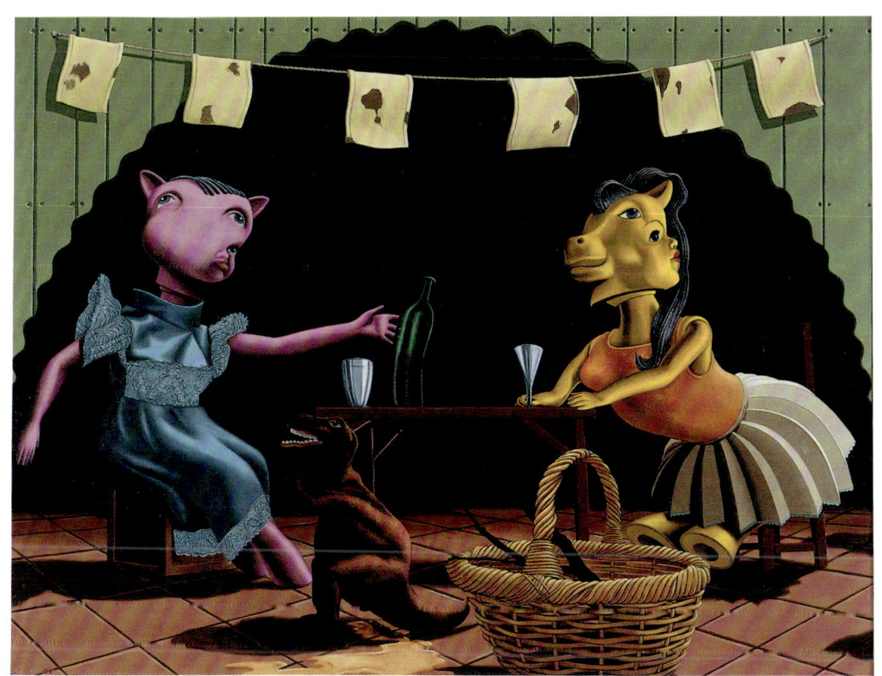

SONIA LAWSON
GRIEVING WOMEN

oil on canvas   152 x 152cm

Sonia Lawson was born in Darlington in 1934. She studied at the Royal College of Art 1956-60. She held her first one-woman show at Zwemmers, London in 1960 and has since exhibited throughout Britain. She has shown regularly at the Royal Academy and was elected ARA in 1982; she became an ARWS in 1984. Major solo shows took place at Milton Keynes (and tour) 1982, Manchester City Art Gallery *(The Midnight Muse)* 1987 and Wakefield/Bradford *(Shrines of Life)* 1988. She has lectured at the Royal College of Art and Royal Academy Schools.

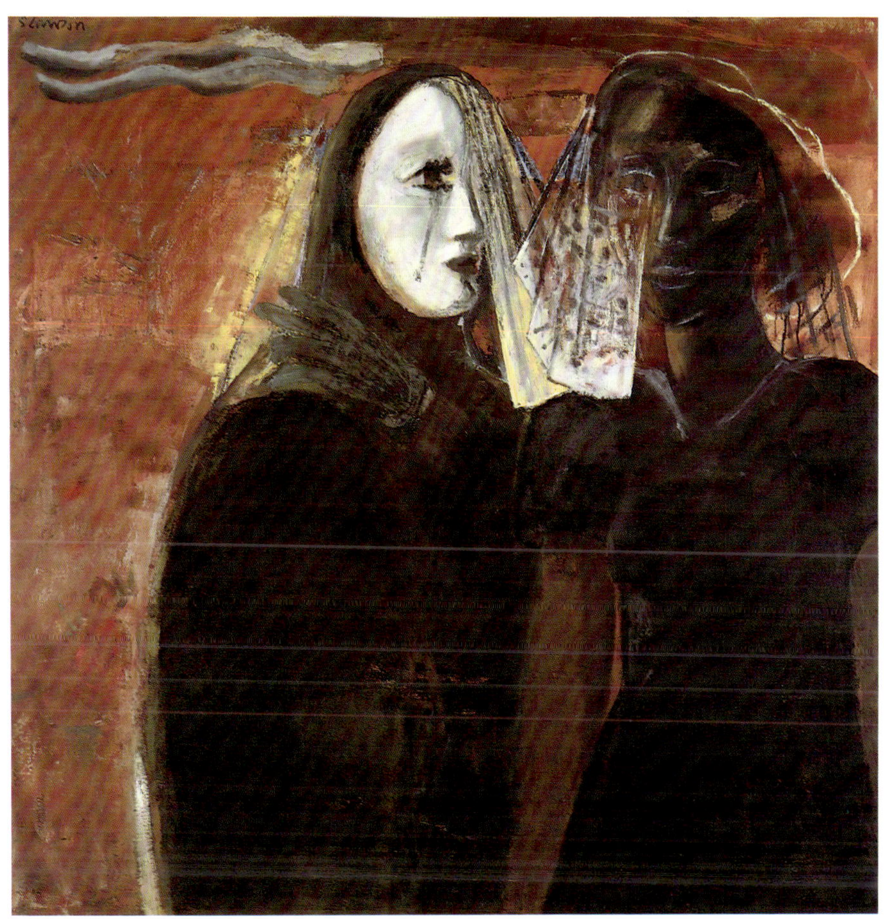

SIMON LING
SIDE A

oil on canvas   183 x 152.5cm

Every moment is completely choreographed
and without meaning. These people are real. The
fan heater is not.

**Simon Ling was born in Bradford in 1968. He
studied at Carmarthen College of Art 1987-88 and
at Chelsea College of Art 1988-91.**

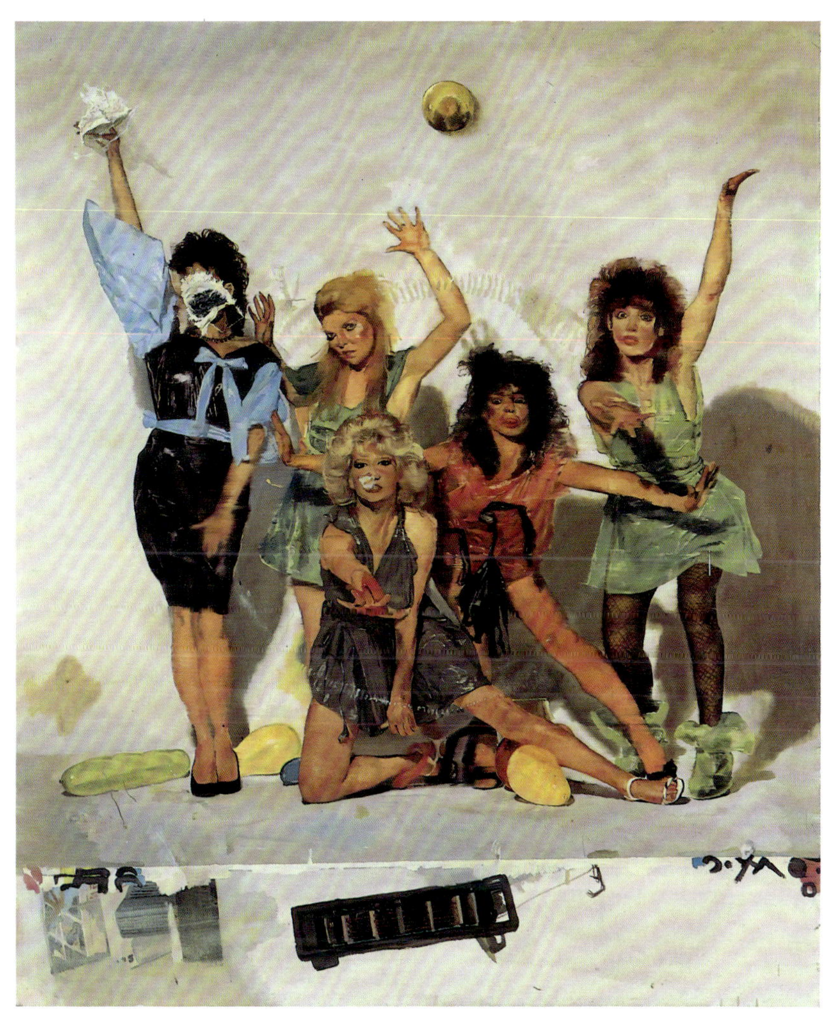

JAMES McDONALD
THE ESTATE AT CARNOCK

oil on wood   103 x 73cm

Carnock was an estate in Stirlingshire, established 500 years ago, which exists now in name only, on old ordnance survey maps. It is an overgrown wilderness, bounded by farmlands and redundant mining villages, and can be reached only by barely discernible footpaths.

This arrangement of decaying books, all split bindings and rotted sellotape, hopefully conveys a sense of impermanence and loss.

James McDonald was born in Stirling in 1956. He studied at Edinburgh College of Art 1974-79. He has exhibited regularly at the Scottish Society of Artists, the Royal Glasgow Institute and the Glasgow Print Studio (including a solo show of paintings and prints in 1989); also at I.C.A.F. London and the Fruitmarket Opens, Edinburgh. Other one-man exhibitions have been at Main Fine Art Glasgow 1986 and Cormund Gallery Glasgow 1991.

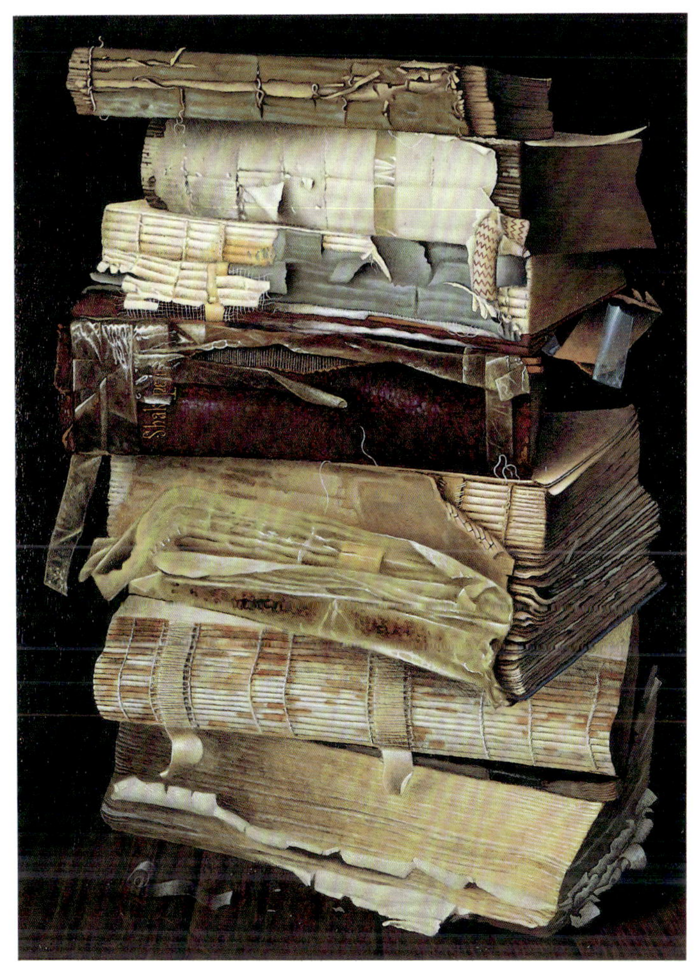

ALAIN MILLER
(FROM HANDS AND EYES) "SHIELD" (1991)

oil on canvas   180.5 x 180.5 cm

Alain Miller was born in London in 1961. He studied at Maidstone College of Art 1979-80, Brighton Polytechnic 1981-84, Chelsea School of Art 1984-85 and Goldsmiths' College 1985-87. His first shows were *Prelude* Kettle's Yard Cambridge 1985 and *New Art 2* Anthony Reynolds Gallery 1985; since then his work has been shown regularly at Anthony Reynolds including one-man shows in 1987 and 1991. His other group shows have included John Moores 15, 1987; the Contemporary Art Society Art Market and 1990 Whitechapel Open.

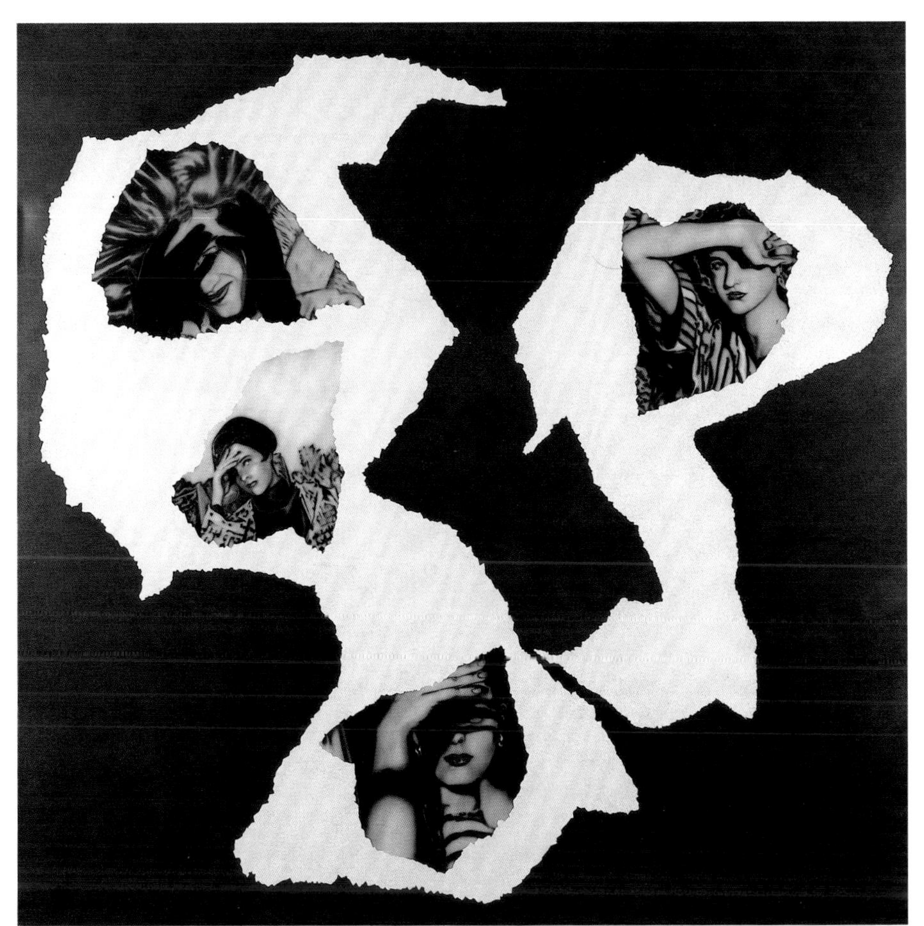

GUY NOBLE
THE SUICIDE

oil on canvas   148 x 153 cm

For the last four years I have been living in Italy - this is the first painting I have completed since my return.

Every subject has a particular way of provoking the imagination and the intellect. When I look at or paint a given subject some aspect of its literal appearance splits away and the content of the painting changes, which in turn feeds my imagination. This transformed content seems to spiral down into what my imagination, my intellect, the subject and the way it appears all compel the painting to become.

Here, although the man jumping off the balcony produces a certain psychological effect, I arrived at this solution while trying to solve what appeared to be essentially formal problems.

The type of painting that interests me most is that which seems to intensify reality. By transforming the literal appearance it gives the image the power to cut deep into the way we see things. The crucial point lies in the way my imagination interacts with the subject and the language I use.

Guy Noble was born in Kent in 1959. He studied at Medway College of Art 1976-77 and the Byam Shaw School 1977-80. He was awarded a Spanish Government Scholarship in 1981-82 and was a National Portrait Gallery Portrait Award winner in 1981 and again in 1984. Since appearing in John Moores 14 in 1985 his shows have included Jablonski Gallery London 1987, Lamont Gallery London 1987 and '91 and Piazza D'Azeglio, Florence 1989. In 1991 he was the Sunday Times/Singer & Friedlander 1st prizewinner.

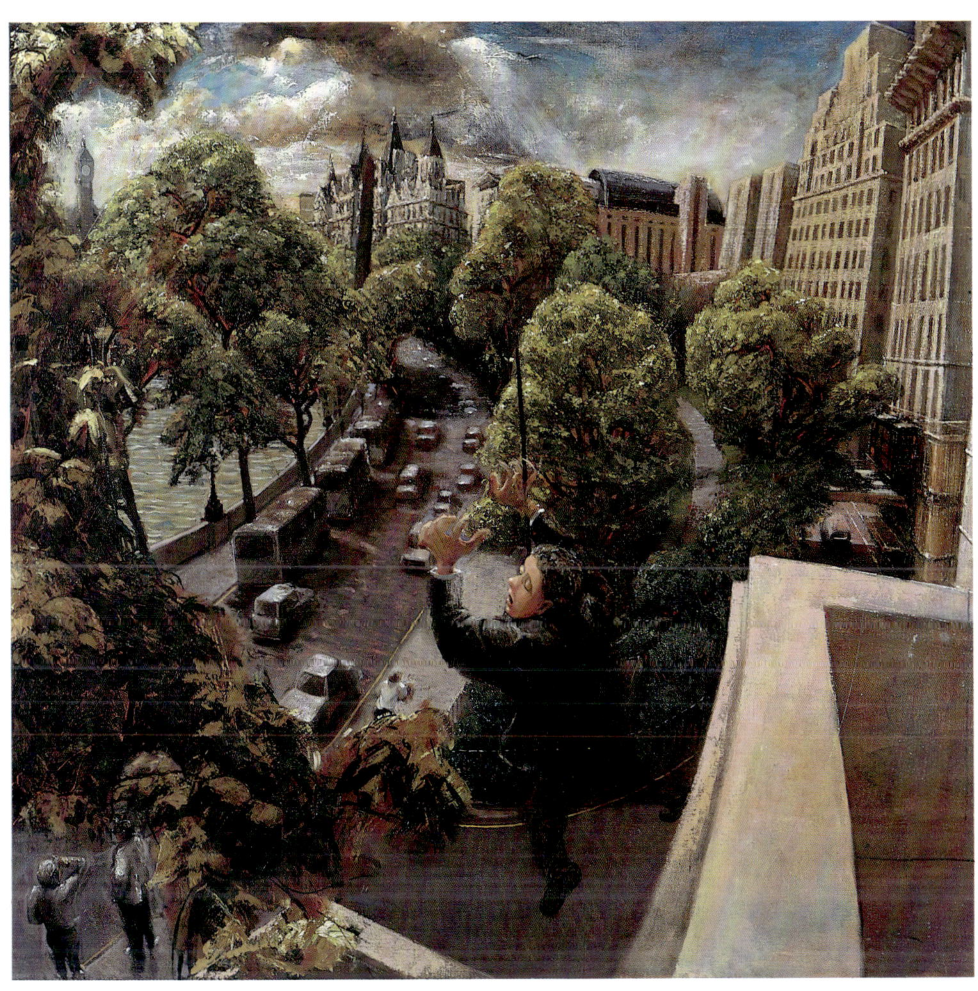

ROY OXLADE
IN THE STUDIO

oil on canvas   130 x 171cm

The more things I can get into my painting the better: the problem is always how to do this free from yesterday's skills and attitudes. At the risk of rawness, even absurdity, I hope that new skills, relevant to my own circumstances, will develop in place of those which are worn out. Topics remain constant and I seem to come back always to the same familiar ones. In *In The Studio* the venetian red ground is as important as anything else. Its colour is a wonderfully receptive bed in which to locate the easels, lamps and model. They settled into their places after many changes. If there are ambiguities they will only be in terms of reference to subject matter. Every nuance of mark, each drip, is there because I want it to be. Like the piece of orange on the left: I'm not sure that it refers to anything except itself, but it is necessary to the painting exactly as it is.

Roy Oxlade was born in London in 1929. He studied at Bromley College of Art 1950-55, and from 1951 to '53 attended David Bomberg's life classes at the Borough Polytechnic. His first group shows were the *Young Contemporaries* 1952, '53 and '54. He spent a period in Canada and held a one-man exhibition at Vancouver Art Gallery 1963. In the same year was his only previous appearance in the John Moores with *Reclining Nude*. His most recent one-man shows have been at the Odette Gilbert Gallery London 1985, '87, and '88 and at the Gardner Centre, University of Sussex, 1990.

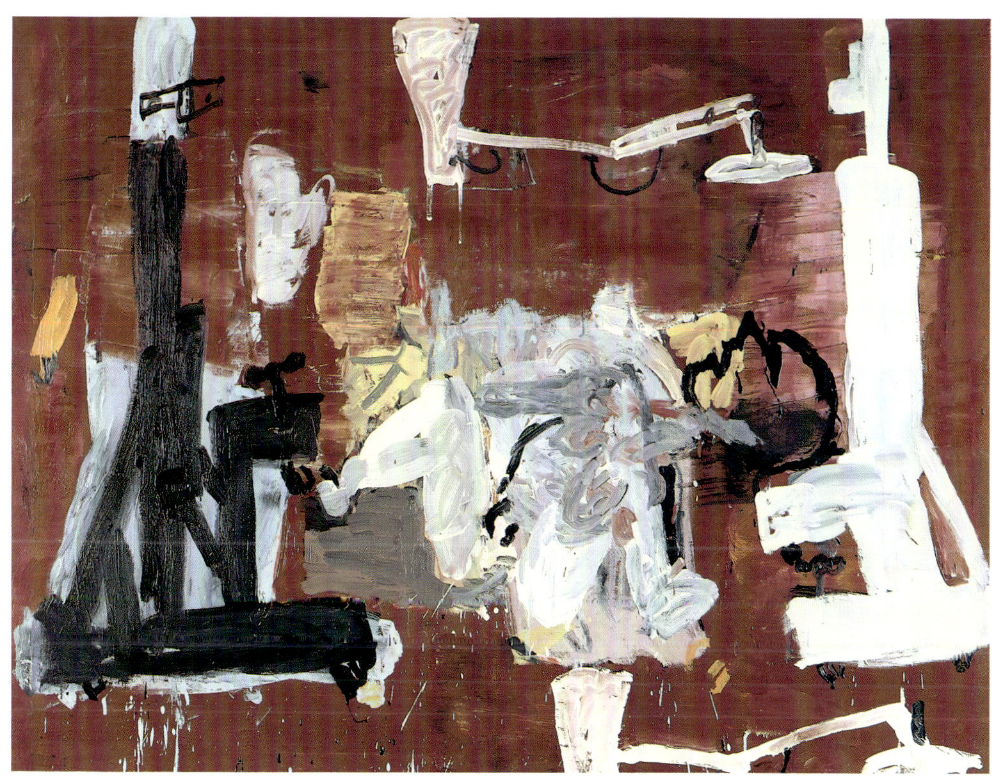

VICTOR PASMORE
BLUE WATER

spray on canvas   243.5 X 201cm

This picture was not intended to represent anything; its form was developed subjectively and independently by moving spray-paint rhythmically over an objective surface from the centre outwards. The final image was called *Blue Water* by spectators who saw it when first exhibited at the Serpentine Gallery in London in April this year. As I like the idea of an abstract painting acquiring a title on its own initiative, so *Blue Water* it will remain.

Victor Pasmore was born in Chelsham, Surrey in 1908. He received no formal art training. After he had established himself as one of Britain's leading figurative painters as a founder of the Euston Road school in the 1930s, his 'conversion' at the end of the 1940s was a key moment in the development of British abstraction. Since his retrospective at the Venice Biennale in 1960 he has exhibited all over the world. He was made CBE in 1959 and CH in 1983. He won 3rd prize in the first John Moores exhibition in 1957 with *Abstract In Black, White, Maroon and Ochre,* his third work to enter the Walker's collection; and this his eleventh John Moores appearance. His most recent retrospective was held at the Serpentine Gallery London in 1991. In 1992 the second volume will appear of the catalogue raisonné of his works, covering the years 1979-91.

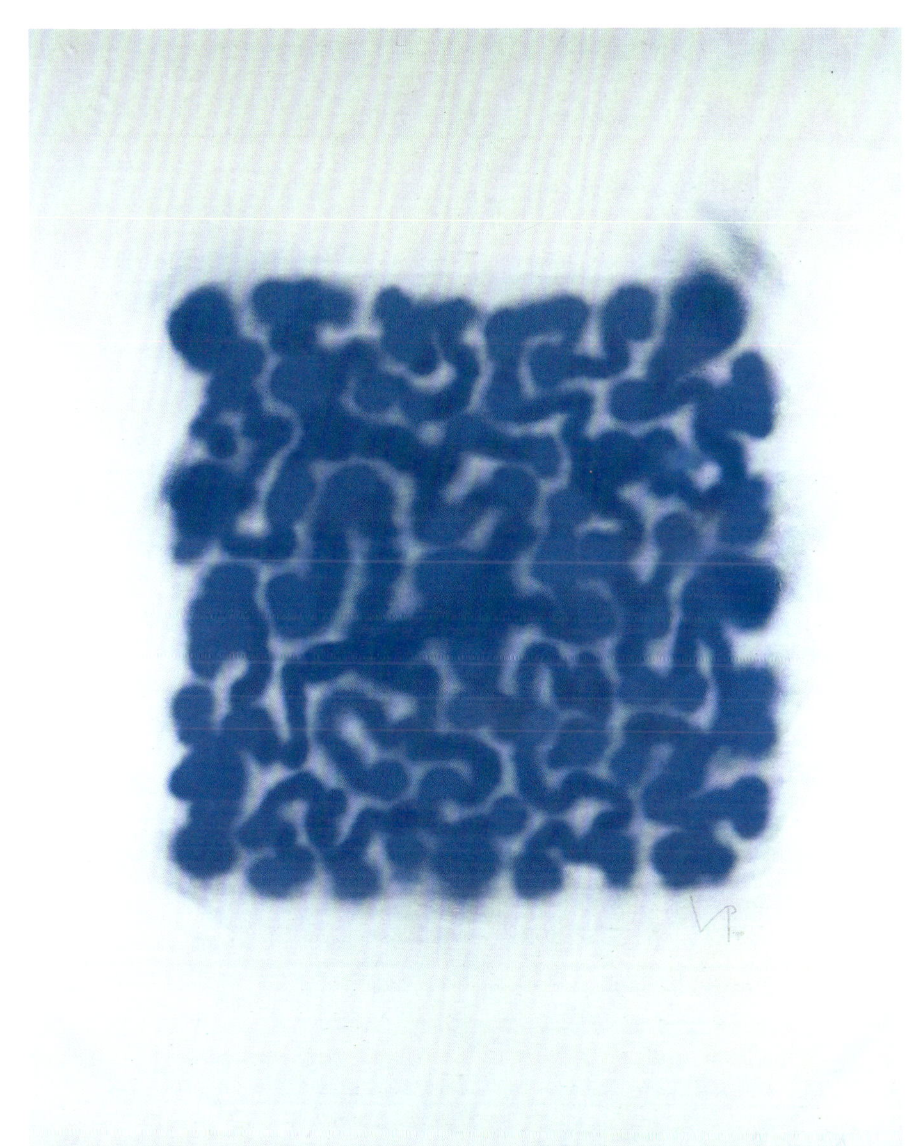

FIONA RAE
UNTITLED (ORANGE GREEN AND BLACK I)

oil on canvas   213.5 x 198 cm

Fiona Rae was born in Hong Kong in 1963. She
studied at Croydon College of Art 1983-84 and
Goldsmiths' College 1984-87. Her first shows were
Freeze, London Docklands 1988 and *Promises
Promises,* Serpentine Gallery London and Ecole de
Nîmes 1989. In 1990 she appeared in *The British Art
Show* Glasgow, and *Aperto* at the Venice Biennale
and had a solo show at the Third Eye Centre,
Glasgow; 1991 exhibitions include Waddington
Galleries London (solo); *Who Framed Modern Art?,*
Sidney Janis New York, *A View of London* Salzburg
Kunstverein, and *British Art From 1930*, Waddington
Galleries. She was nominated for the 1991 Turner
Prize and her work will be seen at the exhibition of
shortlisted artists' work at the Tate Gallery London in
November.

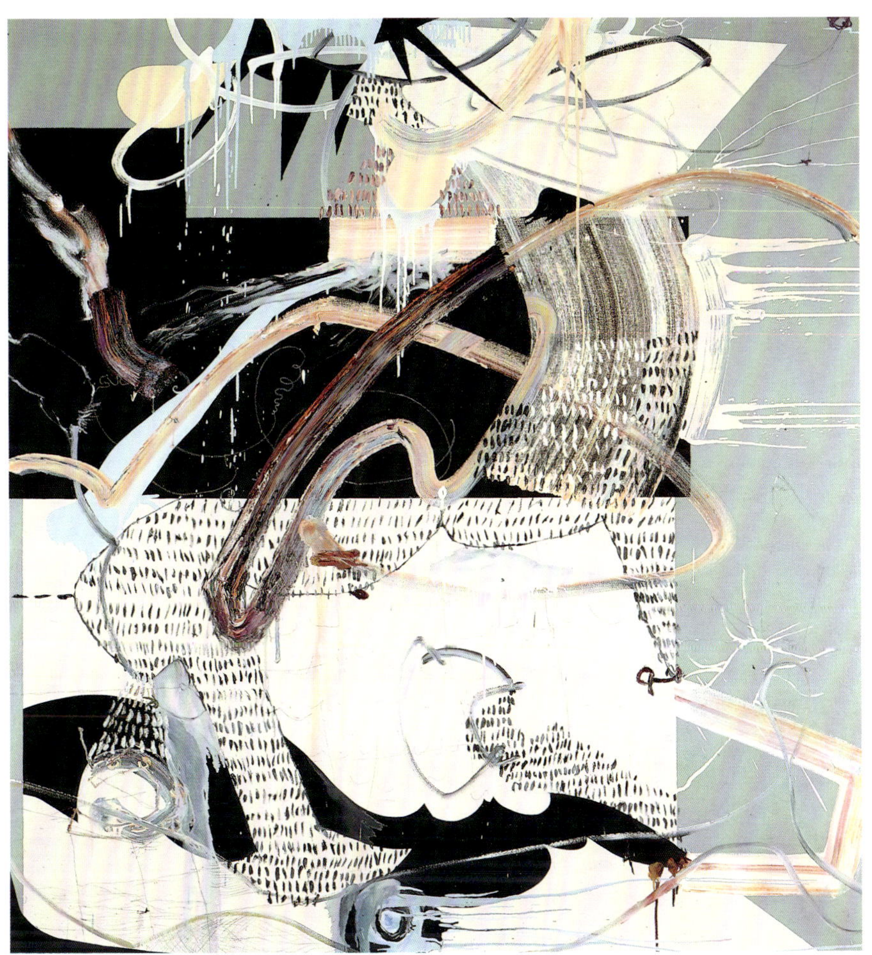

ADRIAN RICHARDSON
BASSARTA

acrylic on canvas   118 x 76 cm

My paintings try to balance the physical, 'matter-of-fact' aspect of paint with its capacity for illusion. I want them to appear both graphic and painterly, both raw and controlled.

Adrian Richardson was born in Birkenhead in 1950. He studied at the Architectural Association School 1969-71, St Martin's School of Art 1971-74 and the Slade School 1974-76. He divides his time between Cairo, where he held one-man exhibitions at ECICC Gallery 1987 and Atelier Du Caire 1988, and London, where his most recent one-man shows have been at Zoo, Islington, 1988 and Black Bull Gallery, Fulham, 1990.

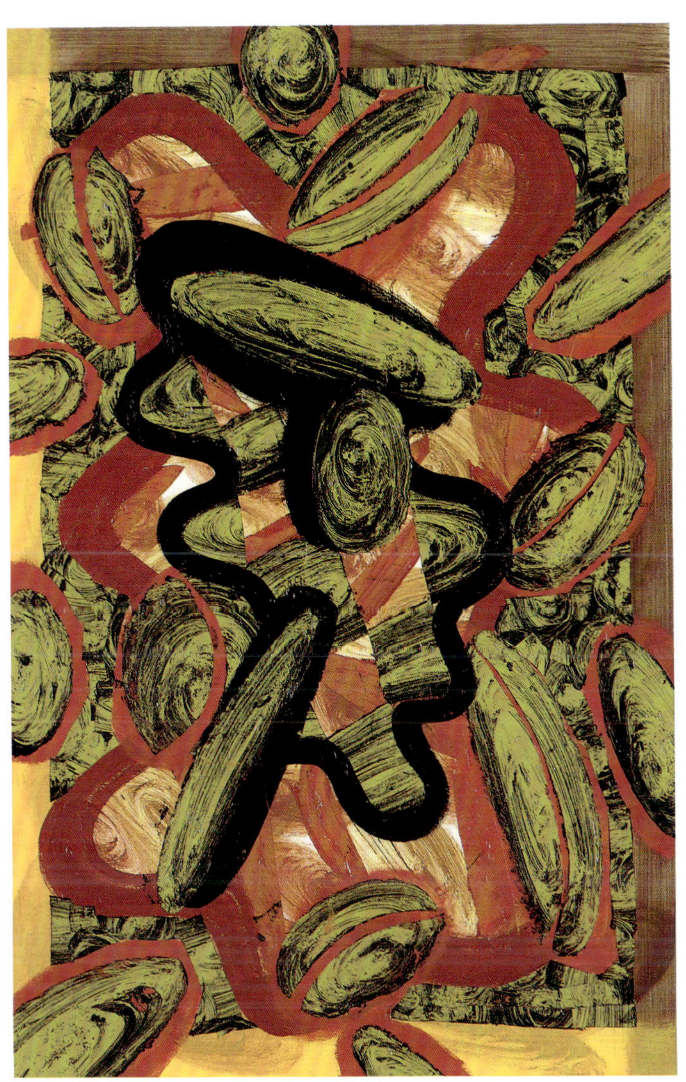

MARIO ROSSI
FREEZE FRAME NO. 8

acrylic on canvas   183 x 213.5cm

Mario Rossi was born in Glasgow in 1958. He studied at Glasgow School of Art 1975-77 and at the Royal College of Art 1979-81. He was Gulbenkian Rome Scholar 1982-83, at the British School at Rome. His first solo show was at the City Art Centre Edinburgh 1984, and he was included in *New Image Glasgow,* Third Eye Centre 1985. Recent major exhibitions have included solo shows at Anderson O'Day London 1988 and '90, Trinity College Cambridge 1989, (marking the end of his two-year Fellowship in Creative Arts), and Oldham Art Gallery 1991; group shows include *Scottish Art Since 1900,* Scottish National Gallery of Modern Art 1989, John Moores 16 1989, *Real Life Stories,* Spacex Exeter 1990 and *Post Morality,* Kettle's Yard Cambridge 1990. He is visiting lecturer at Goldsmiths' College London.

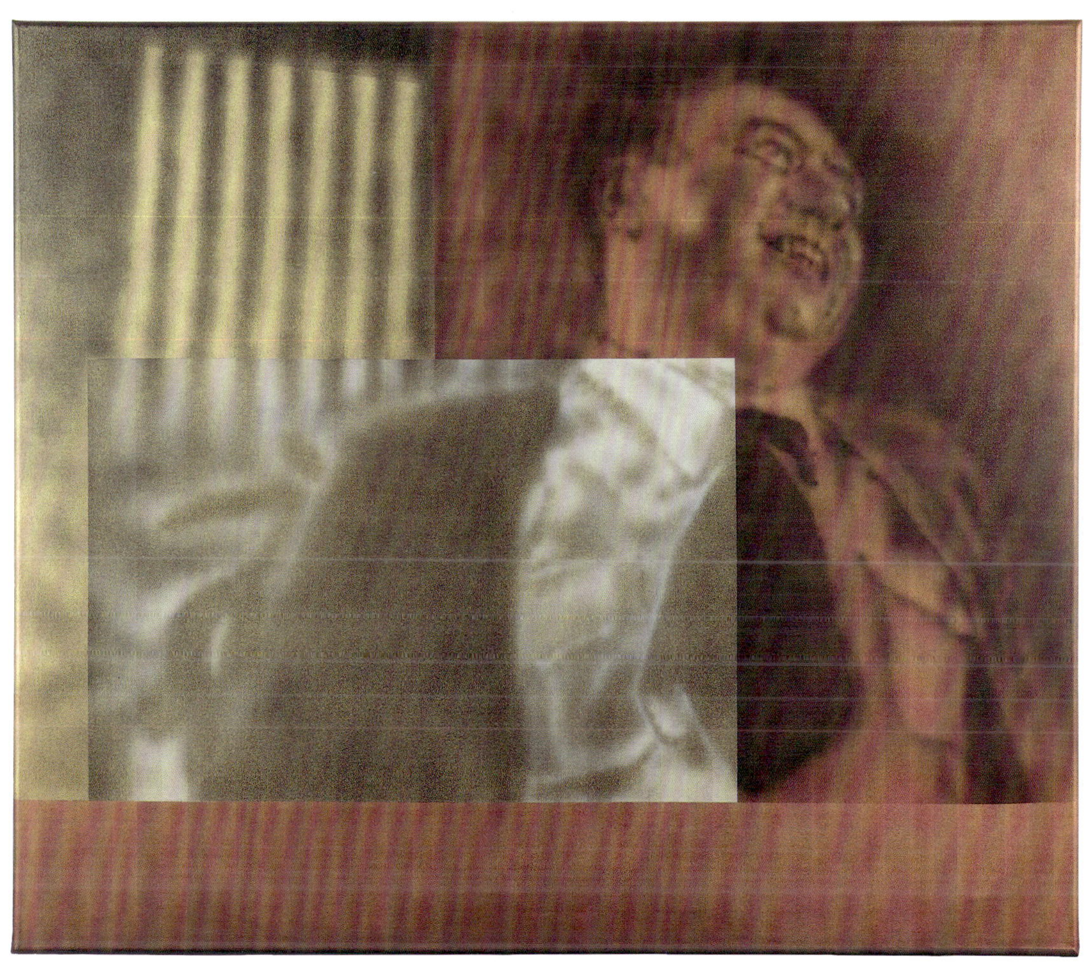

KEVIN SINNOTT
THE ARTIST AND HIS MUSICIANS

oil on canvas   215.5 x 159.5cm

The musicians gather behind the artist, pressing him to work perhaps. Palette in hand he looks out and beyond. The Muses have come to visit along with influences and biographical forces. Behind are to be found Picasso's Musicians from 1925 - creating a difficult contrast in styles but also suggesting the many turns and changes that make up our (or his) fragmented times and artistic context.

I hoped that the inclusion of the Picasso in the background would confound the 'historicist' view of art and its linear development.

Kevin Sinnott was born in Wales in 1947. He studied at Cardiff College of Art 1967-68, Gloucester College of Art 1968-71 and The Royal College of Art 1971-74. Among his first group shows were John Moores 11 and 12, 1978 and '80, in the second of which he won a prize. His first one-man show was at the House Gallery London 1980, since when he has exhibited regularly in London and Oxford and also in the USA. He has taught at the Ruskin School, Canterbury College and St Martin's School of Art.

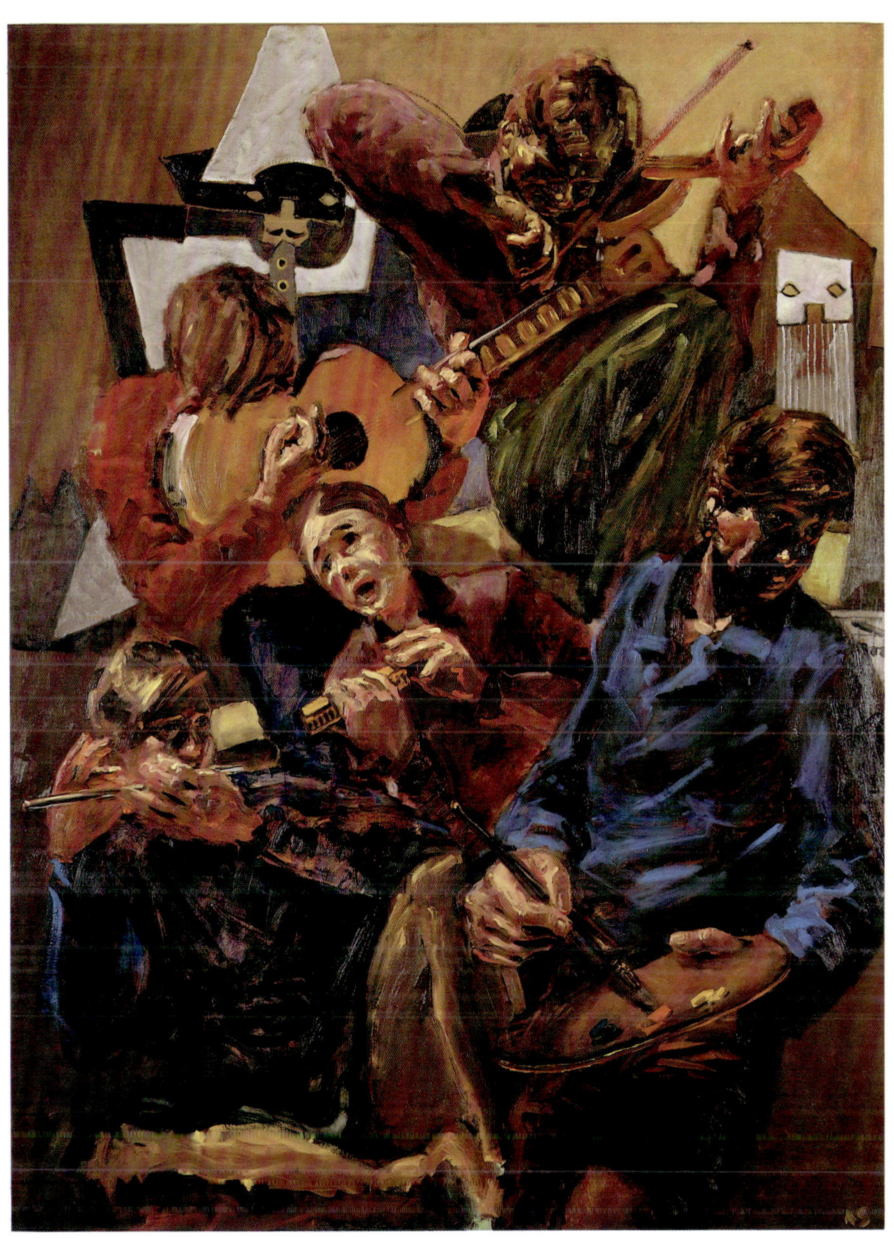

MARK SKINNER
DOVE TALE

oil and enamel on board   181 x 122 cm

The starting point for much of my work is physical and ideological conflict. This picture stems from a series of nine drawings depicting the escalating stages of a struggle between two forces, one essentially suppressive, the other increasingly anarchic.

Mark Skinner was born in Liverpool in 1957. He studied at Liverpool Polytechnic 1976-77 and Birmingham Polytechnic 1977-80. His exhibitions include *The First Picture Show*, Sainsbury Centre Norwich 1981; Bluecoat Gallery 1983 and 1988; University of Liverpool 1986, ICA, London 1987, and Merkmal Gallery Liverpool 1991. A one-man show is projected for the Arts Council of Northern Ireland Gallery, Belfast.

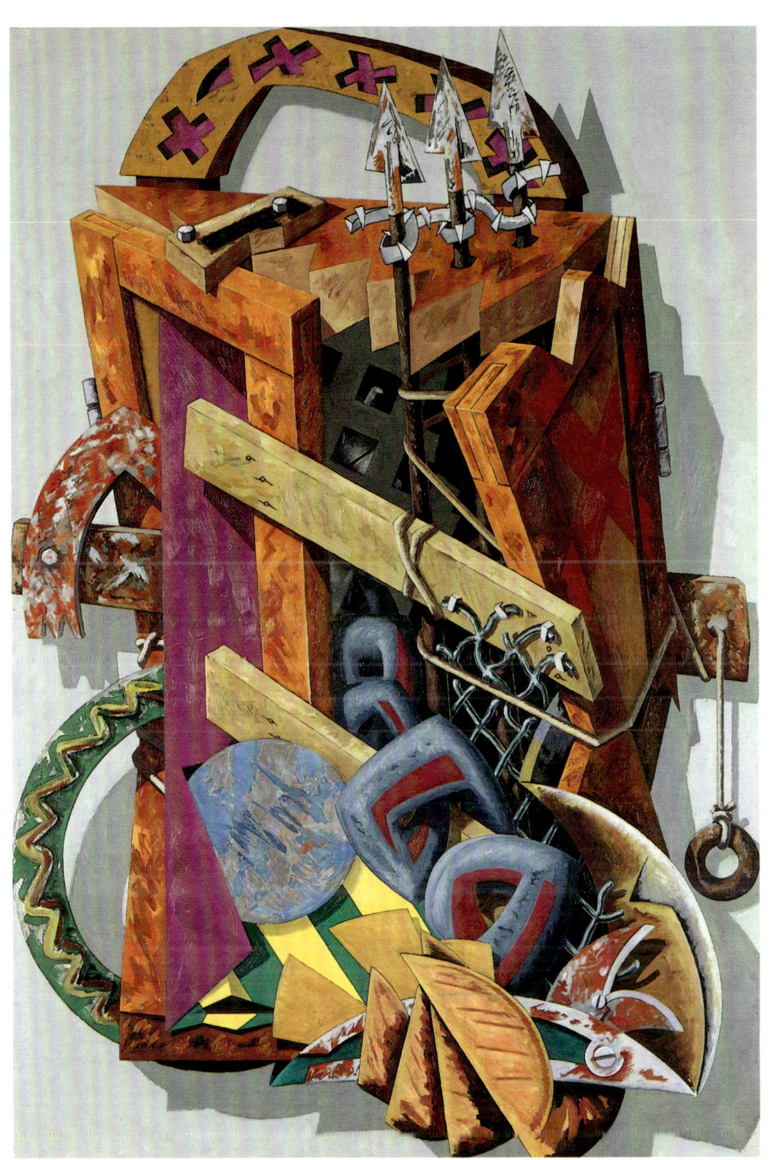

JOE TILSON
DEMETER

oil on canvas on wood relief   221 x 221cm

Joe Tilson was born in London in 1928. He studied at St Martin's School of Art 1949-52 and the Royal College of Art 1952-55. One of his earliest group shows was the 1st John Moores, 1957, at which he won a £25 prize; he won 3rd prize in 1967 and this is his eighth appearance in the show. Since his first one-man show in London in 1962 he has exhibited all over the world both as painter and printmaker; he has appeared regularly in the Bradford Print Biennale and the Ljubljana Print International at which he has won major prizes. Among his shows in 1991 are *Pop Prints,* Tate Gallery London, *British Art From 1930,* Waddington Galleries London, and the Royal Academy's *Pop Art* exhibition. Three of his works are in the Walker Art Gallery collection.

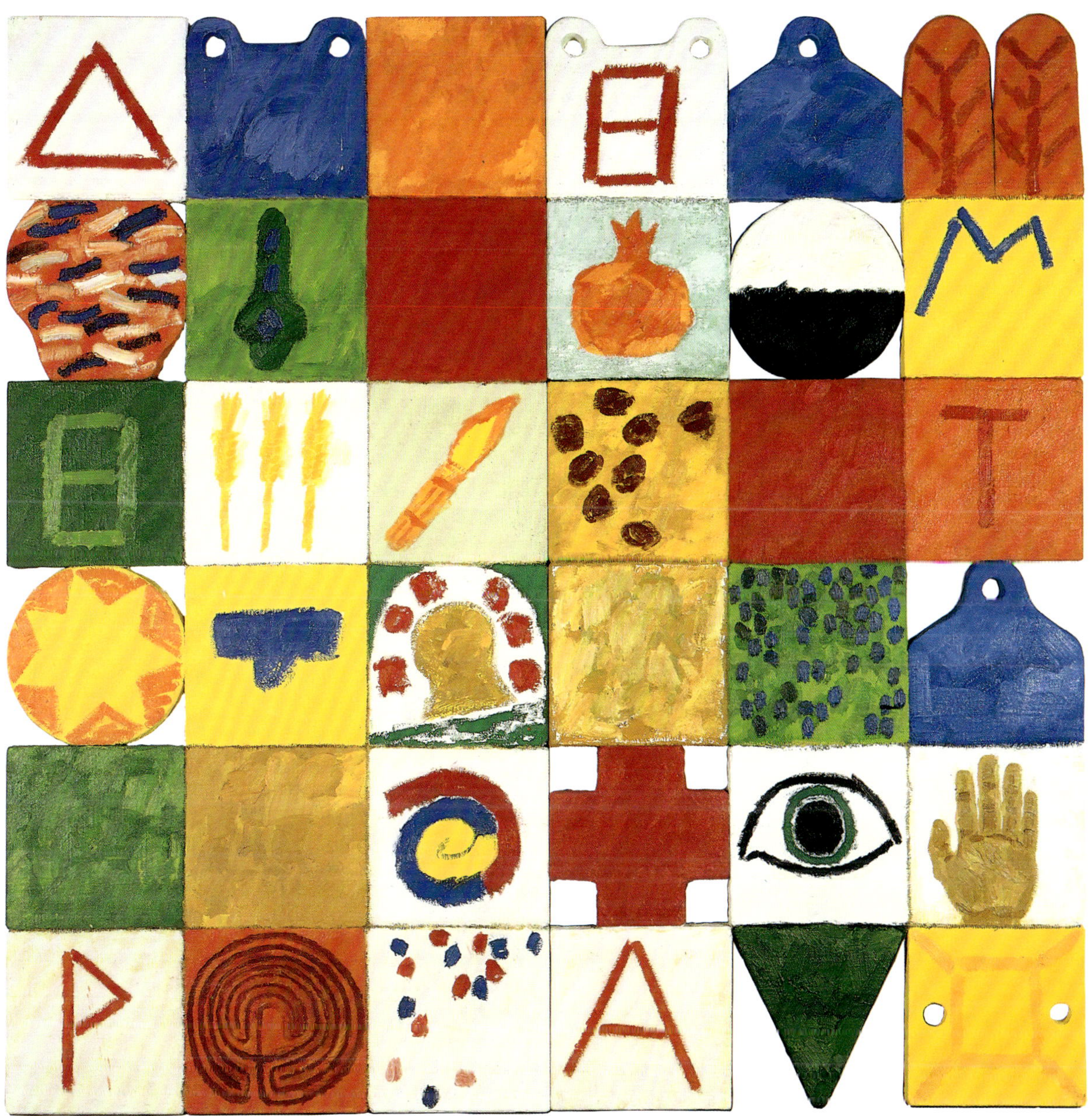

PIERS WARDLE

MITCHELSON-MORLEY

acrylic on canvas   202.5 x 291 cm

When an image reaches a certain level of complexity without presenting an obvious structure of meaning (e.g. the patterns made by paint peeling off a wall) it can be described as fractal or as having a chaotic structure. The perceptual system of a human being, however, is anti-chaotic; capable of resolving complexity into meaning. We see faces in the fire or Jesus in the clouds; maybe representation began in an attempt to augment an image glimpsed in the patterns on a rock, as a kind of divination.

Living in the city we are bombarded with visual information, which as well as disappearing when of no further use can become jumbled, fragmented and partially obliterated in a cumulative process whereby once clear and deliberate meanings re-combine into something more complex and less definite.

For example there is a sort of tide-line at the edge of the pavement, blown there by passing traffic, consisting of dust, sand, plastic wrappers, spilt paint, car parts and occasionally something arresting and unusual like a child's drawing. The whole simultaneously invites interpretation and denies it.

In this painting I try for a similar level of saturation, beyond the point where the surface has become 'used up', to where a single reading becomes problematic and many may be possible.

Piers Wardle was born in Beckenham, Kent in 1960. He studied at Exeter College of Art 1976-77 and the Ruskin School 1977-80. His first major shows were at the ACME Gallery London 1981 and MOMA Oxford 1982. Since then he has exhibited in London at the Pomeroy Purdy Gallery, the Crypt, and the Bernard Baron Gallery; and at the Eastbourne Clark Gallery Florida, 1990.

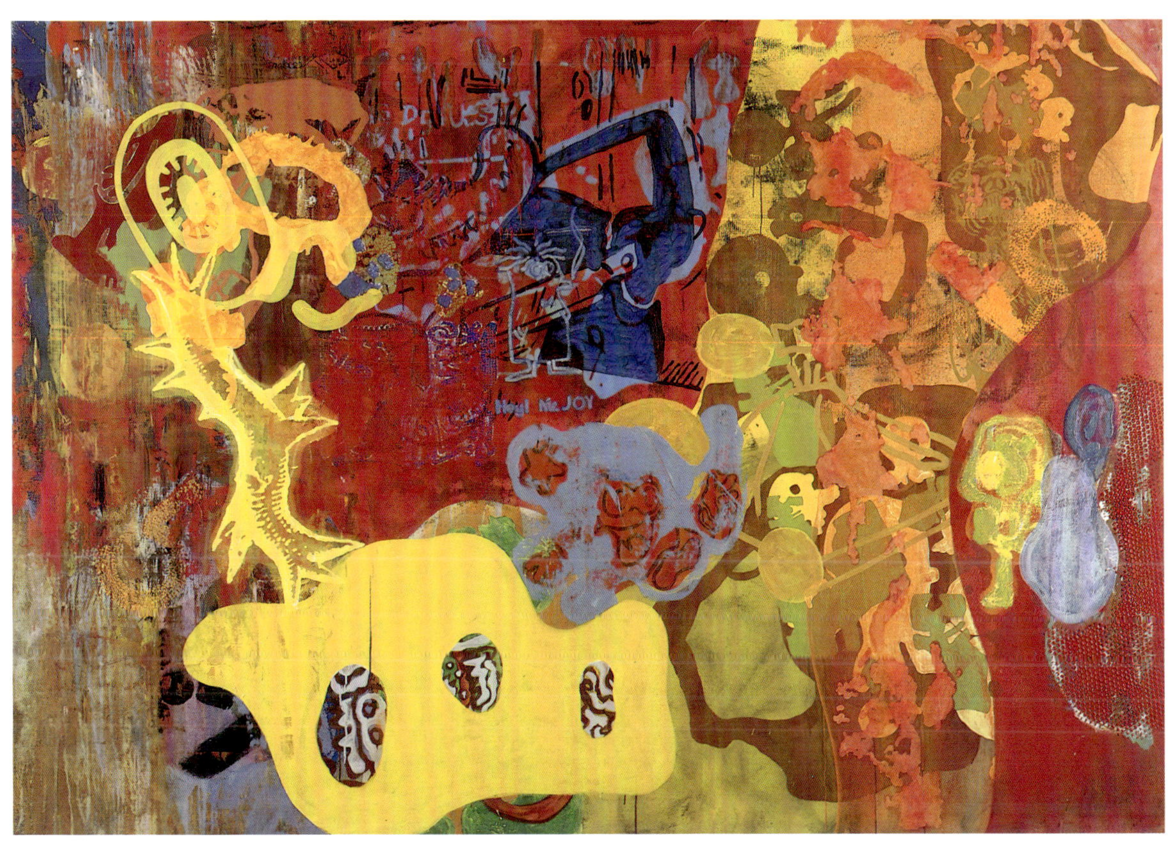

Hey! Mr. JOY

ALAN WELSFORD
VIGILANT RESOLUTION

oil on canvas   198 x 305 cm

This is a recent painting on a longstanding and ongoing theme entitled 'In Defence of the Realm'. The theme is ironic, humorous and political in flavour.

This particular work comes from a large group which uses ideas and imagery based on submarines.

The Polaris submarine *Resolution* has become something of an obsession. Especially the idea of the name; but I am also intrigued by the notion of this vast, lethal electronic guardian patrolling secretly and silently in the mysterious depths of the sea. A glowing, humming, hermetic world...a jungle of instruments, of dials, screens, pipes, tubes and flashing lights...a twenty-four hour deadly feedback system requiring constant attention.

The subject-matter is a strong motivating force, but equally so are formal problems. I want each painting to work as an interesting and autonomous thing in its own right. The qualities of paint handling, the physicality of the surface and the colour and scale are central to my concerns as a painter.

The painting was worked on for over a year as I gradually changed and developed the image and slowly built up the paint surface.

Alan Welsford was born at Hainault, Essex in 1935. He studied at Walthamstow School of Art 1956-59 and at the Slade School 1959-63. He won the Rome Prize and spent the following year at the British School in Rome. His painting *Televised Floodlight Game* won a prize in John Moores 4 1963 and was purchased by the Walker Art Gallery. While exhibiting regularly in group shows as a painter he developed parallel careers as a sculptor and more recently in film, and since 1984 he has participated regularly in film festivals nationally and internationally. He is currently Course Leader in Fine Art at Leicester Polytechnic.

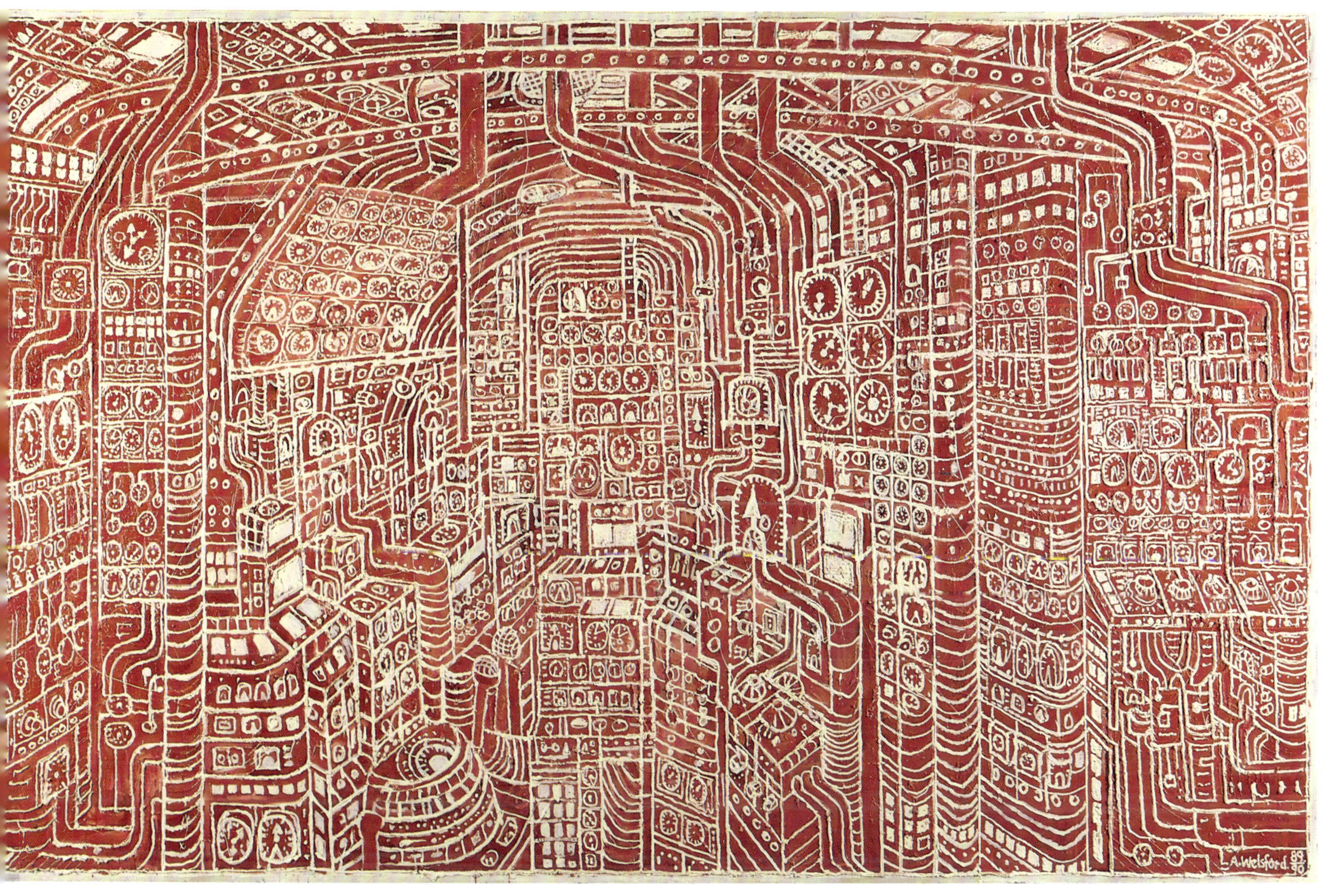

SUZANNE WILLEY
UNTITLED

oil on canvas   40.5 x 30.5; 40.5 x 30.5 cm

I have been using found images for some time and recently have taken images from Hergé's *Tintin*. These provide a model with which to work that can be articulated on different levels: references in the subject matter which are humorous and instantly recognizable; but also I hope a concentration on the more formal considerations with painting as the real subject matter.

Suzanne Willey was born in London in 1961. She studied at Bath Academy of Art 1981-84 and Goldsmiths' College 1986-88. She appeared in the Whitechapel Open 1987, in group shows at the Air Gallery and at Anderson O'Day, London, 1988, and in 1990 in The London Group, The Royal Overseas League *View of the New, Into the 90s* at the Mall Galleries and Austin Desmond's Christmas show.

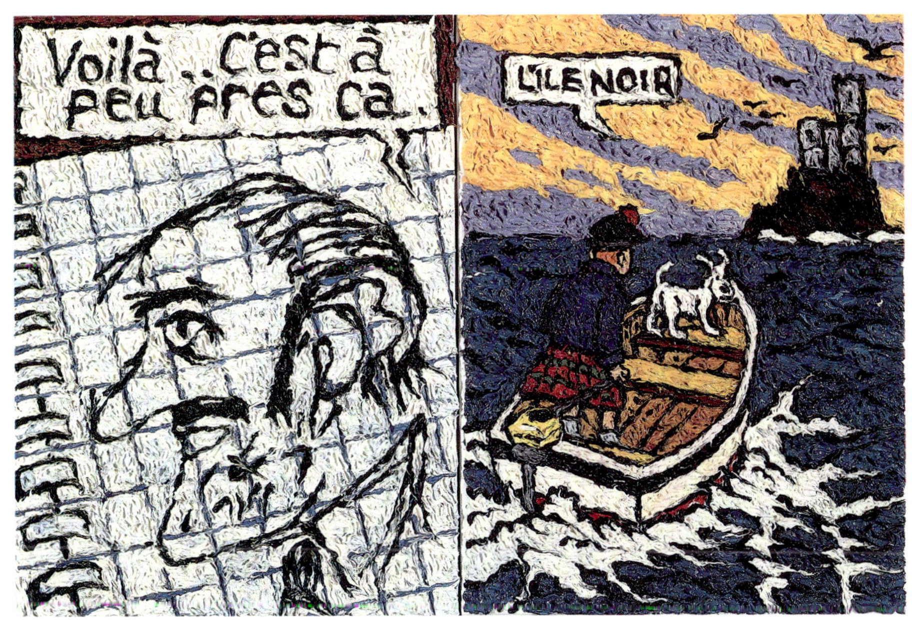
Voilà .. C'est à
peu près ça.
L'ILE NOIR

GARY WRAGG
THE GAP III

oil on canvas   251.5 x 320 cm

A loose geometry of marks was gradually worked into the initial layers of thin stains of primary reds, yellows and blues and light purples, off-whites and pinks. Intensity and solidity of colour built up as the painting developed. The various permutations of mixtures culminated after half a year into bronze, olive greens and browns. The introduction of juicy crimson paint led to a spread of darker re-inforced colours and the initial geometry exploded and dissolved into rhythmic vertical linear divisions, intervals and circular enclosures. By playing around with coloured areas, linear brush marks, forms and division of areas, an essential emphasis of interval evolved.

I have always had a fascination with certain greens. This was the colour that dominated not only *Gap III* but the whole series of *Gap* paintings of 1990. While it is natural for complex imagery to stimulate external associations, the emphasis of balance for me is that the painting is independent of exterior attachments, and exists in its own right. My interest in the gap in the fence outside my studio window triggered numerous internal reactions.

Gary Wragg was born in High Wycombe in 1946. He studied at High Wycombe School of Art 1962-66, Camberwell School 1966-69 and the Slade School 1969-71. He won a Boise scholarship to the USA and Mexico 1972. His first one-man show was at the ACME Gallery London 1976. He showed in *Recent British Painting* 1974 at the Hayward Gallery and *British Painting 1952-77* at the Royal Academy; major shows in the 1980s included the Sydney Biennale 1982 and one-man shows at Nicola Jacobs, London 1982 and 1986. In recent years he has appeared regularly in London Group shows at the RCA and at the Royal Academy Summer Exhibition, and his most recent one-man exhibition was at Goldsmiths' Gallery London 1990.

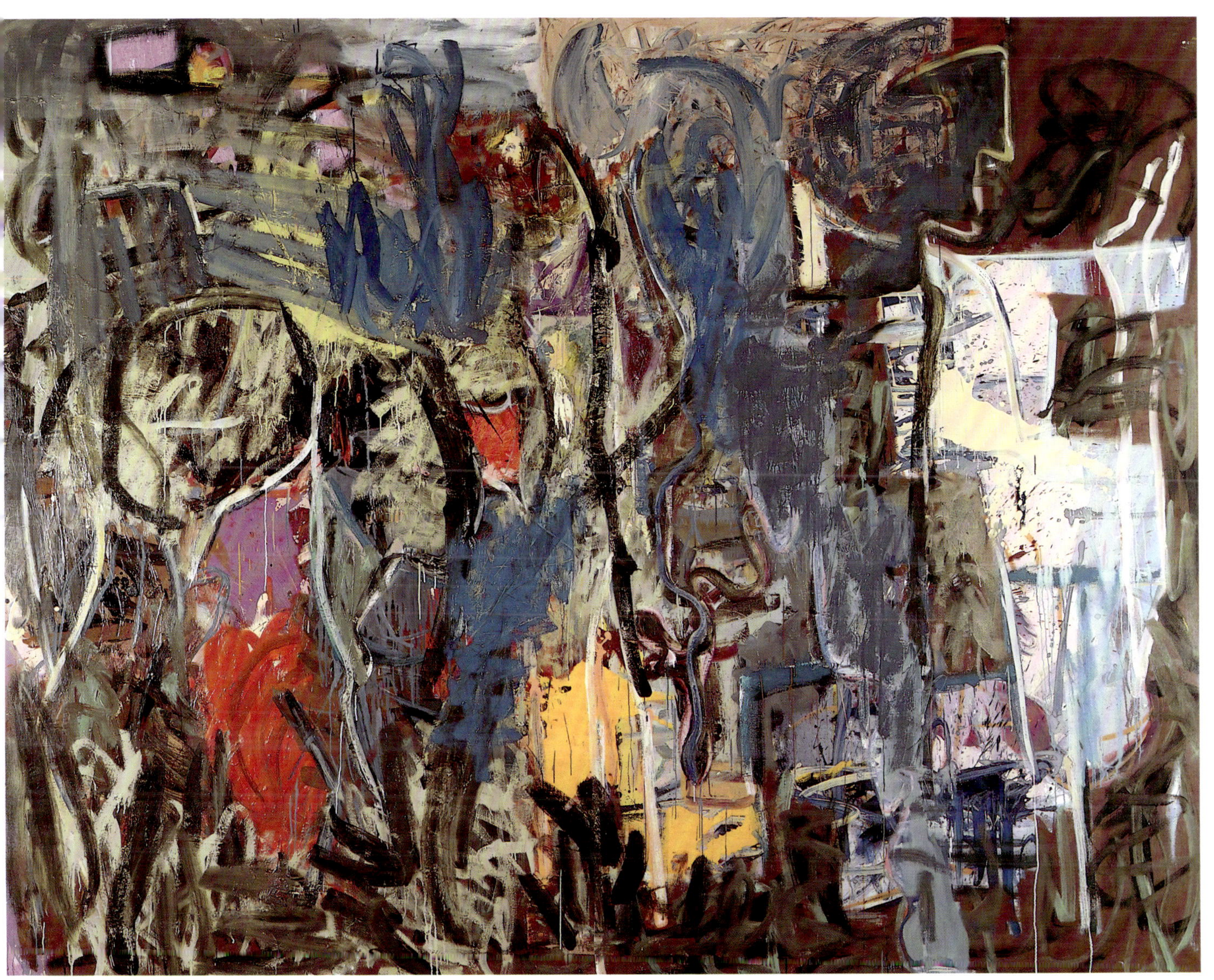

ROSE WYLIE
ARTIST IN STUDIO WITH STOVE, SOFA, PLAN CHEST AND DRAPE

oil on canvas   152.5 x 182 cm

Usually I have to like the look of the thing I'm painting in some way or another. I don't like arty stuff and I don't like photographic realism because I think painting is a transforming process where materials and subject take on new life together. At the same time I do want some sort of likeness. Here, I've put the artist in the colour he most often wears; I've used the dark red of the stove and the news-papers which are spread on the floor.

I work from observation and memory and begin with the colour and forms things are, but anything may change as the work goes on.

I made lots of drawings before I began this stu-dio painting. The sofa was a problem until I put the back rest on its opposite side. Earlier, the sofa had been a large paint brush.

I paint and draw flat on the floor and stretch up a painting only when it's finished.

Rose Wylie was born in Hythe, Kent, in 1934. She studied at Folkestone School of Art 1952-56 and at the Royal College of Art 1979-81. Her exhibitions include the Hayward Annual 1982; the Cleveland International Drawing Biennale 1985; a one-woman show at the Trinity Arts Centre, Tunbridge Wells 1985; two group shows at Odette Gilbert Gallery London 1988; and *David Bomberg and Others*, Towner Gallery Eastbourne 1991.

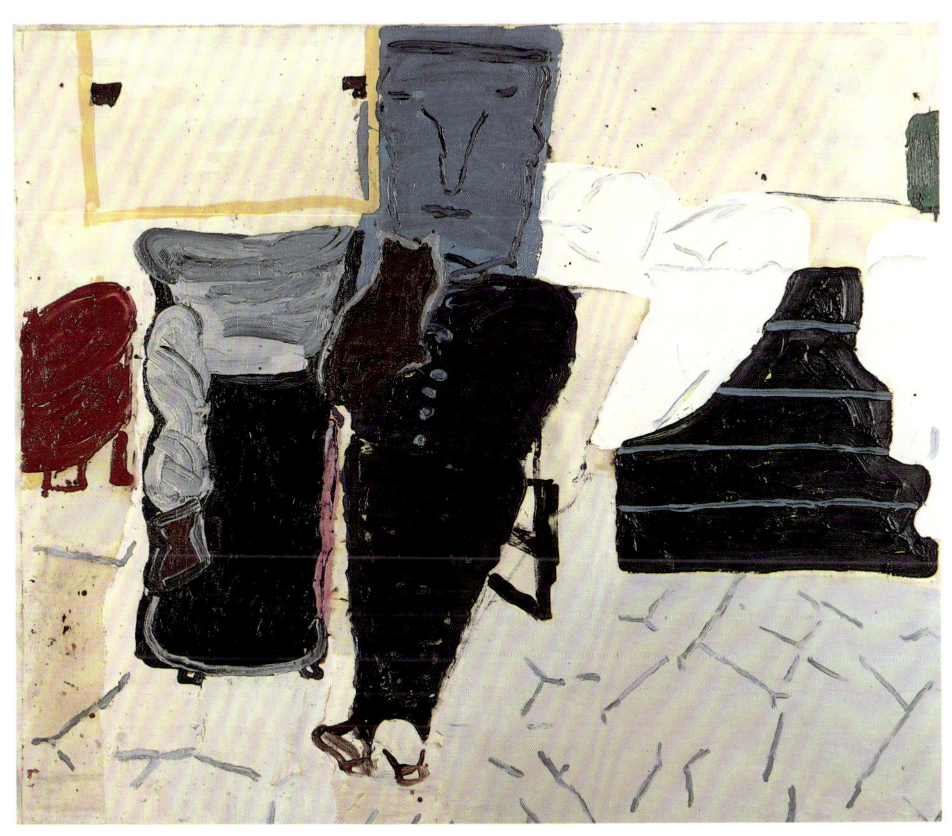

RICHARD YOUNG
DRAWINGS ON THE WALL

oil on canvas   152.5 x 122cm

The content is twenty five self-portrait drawings. They date from 1948 to 1988.

During the process of painting, I became interested in the ageing coloration of the paper: some drawings fading with the onset of time.

The painting was made during 1990.

Richard Young was born in Walton, Liverpool in 1921. He studied part time at Liverpool Art College night classes and returned to study at Liverpool Polytechnic 1979-82. He was a regular exhibitor at the Liverpool Academy and elsewhere in the North-West during the 1960s when two of his works, *Chandelier* and *Interior with Figure* were purchased by the Walker Art Gallery. Group shows in the 1980s included Riverside Gallery London 1981, Hayward Annual 1982 *(British Drawing)*, Royal Academy 1986 and Ayling Porteous Chester 1988; and he held numerous one-man and group shows in Liverpool at the Bluecoat, Bridewell, Acorn and Merkmal Galleries. This is his first appearance in the John Moores exhibition.

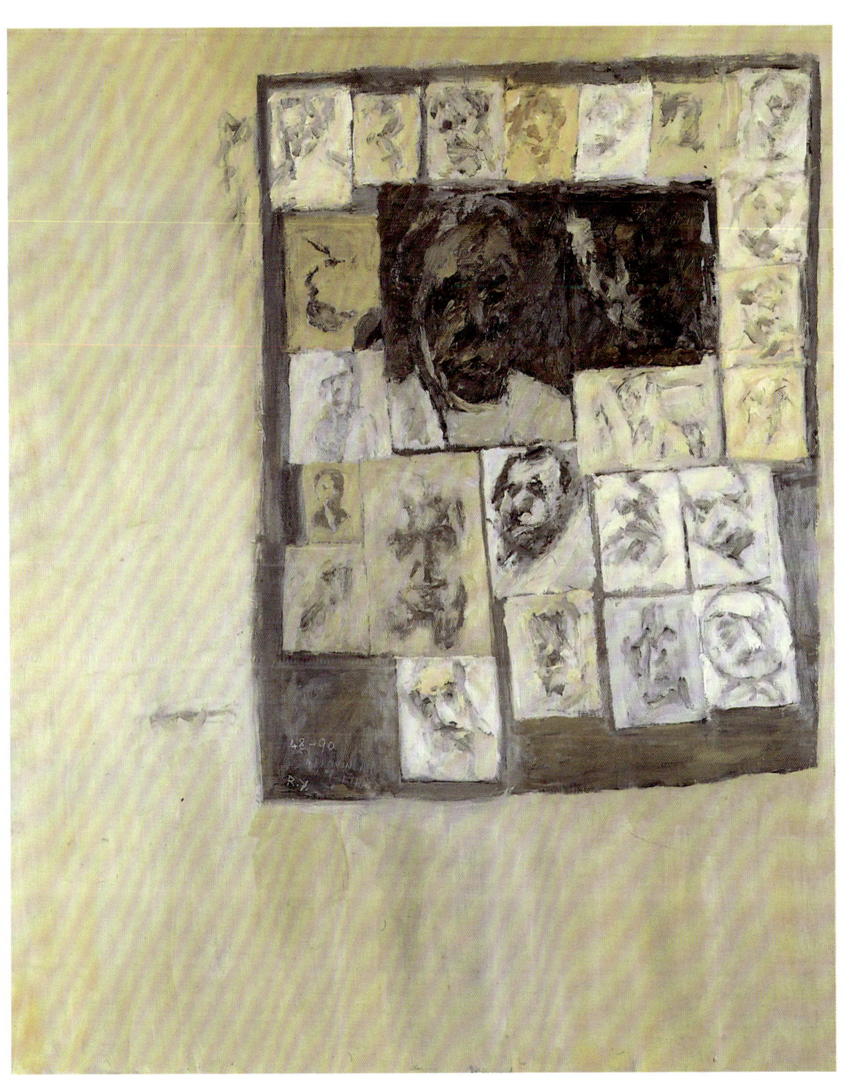

ADAMS Will 7 Bruce Road, Bow, London, E3 3HN
BEATTIE Basil Flat 1, 3 Drakefield Road, Tooting, London, SW17 8RT
BICKNELL John c/o Pomeroy Purdy Gallery, Jacob St Studios, Mill Street, London, SE1 2BA
BRONZIN Licia 25 Barham House, Kinglake Street, London, SE17 2LQ
BROOK James 142 Old Woolwich Road, London, SE10 9PR
CAPSTACK John 6 Ash Grove, Leeds, West Yorkshire, LS6 1AY
CHORLTON Graham 9 Pineapple Grove, Stirchley, Birmingham, B30 2TJ
CLAUSEN Rupert 61b De Beauvoir Road, London N1
CLOSSICK Peter 358 Lee High Road, Lee Green, London, SE12 8RS
COLVERT Brendan Closes Farm, Longsplatt, Kingsdown, Wiltshire, SN14 9DG
DELLOW Jeff 43 Gordonbrock Road, Brockley, London, SE4 1JA
DI STEFANO Arturo c/o Pomeroy Purdy Gallery, Jacob St Studios, Mill Street, London, SE1 2BA
DUFFY Terry BADA, 82/84 Duke Street, Liverpool, L1 5AA
FARTHING Stephen Ruskin School of Drawing, 74 High Street, Oxford, OX1 4BG
GILLMAN Tricia 149 Algernon Road, London, SE13 7AP
GODFREY-ISAACS Laura 40 Crewdson Road, London SW9
GREENLAND Martin 5 Highfield Road, Sedbergh, Cumbria, LA10 5DH
HALLIDAY Trevor Belmont House, 31 Bargate, Grimsby, South Humberside
HAMLYN Paul 61 Etta Street, Deptford, London, SE8 5NR
HAMMOND Joel 25 Linden Mansions, Hornsey Lane, London N6
HAMPER Nichollas 16 Templar Road, Oxford, OX2 8LT
HOUSLEY Paul Blast Lane Studios, Blast Lane, Sipelia Works, Sheffield
HUBBARD John Chilcombe House, Chilcombe, Nr Bridport, Dorset, DT6 4PN
INSHAW David c/o Waddington Galleries, 11 Cork Street, London, W1X 1PD
IRVIN Albert c/o Gimpel Fils, 30 Davies Street, London, W1Y 1LG
JACKOWSKI Andrzej c/o Marlborough Fine Art (London) Ltd., 6 Albemarle Street, London, W1X 4BY
KEMP Richard 58 Juniper House, Pomeroy Street, London, SE14 5BY
KHAN Unit 2, 650 Holloway Road, London N19
KNOWLES Mike Glanaber, Penysarn, Amlwch, Anglesey, Gwynedd
LANSLEY Andrea 10 Church Road, West Kirby, Wirral, Merseyside, L48 0RW
LARSEN Dirk 9 Oakfield Place, Bristol, Avon, BS8 2BJ
LAWSON Sonia 39 Stoke Road, Linslade, Leighton Buzzard, Bedfordshire, LU7 7SW
LING Simon Woodbine Farm, Neyland, Dyfed, SA73 1QN
LOWE Adam c/o Pomeroy Purdy Gallery, Jacob St Studios, Mill Street, London, SE1 2BA
McDONALD James 7b Stuart House, Burns Road, Cumbernauld, Scotland, G67 2AN
McFADYEN Jock 284 Globe Road, Bethnal Green, London E2
MILLER Alain 4 Clarence House, Rushcroft Road, London SW2
NOBLE Guy 28 Calvin Street, London, E1 5NP
OXLADE Roy Forge Cottage, Newnham, Sittingbourne, Kent, ME9 0LQ
PASMORE Victor c/o Marlborough Fine Art (London) Ltd., 6 Albemarle Street, London, W1X 4BY
RAE Fiona c/o Waddington Galleries, 11 Cork Street, London, W1X 1PD
RICHARDSON Adrian 1b Oldfield Road, London, N16 0RR
ROSSI Mario 99 Ashfield Street, London, E1 2HA
SIMPSON Michael The Old Gas Works, Frome Road, Bradford on Avon, Wiltshire, BA15 1LE
SINNOTT Kevin 43 Capel Road, East Barnet, Hertfordshire, EN4 8JF
SKINNER Mark Studio 19, Bluecoat Chambers, School Lane, Liverpool, L1 3BX
TILSON Joe c/o Waddington Galleries, 11 Cork Street, London, W1X 1PD
WARDLE Piers 4 Sullivan Road, London, SE11 4UH
WELSFORD Alan 20 Old Mill Road, Broughton Astley, Leicestershire, LE9 6PQ
WILLEY Suzanne Flat 8, Luxborough Tower, Luxborough Street, London, W1M 3LT
WRAGG Gary 14g Randolph Crescent, Maida Vale, London, W9 1DR
WYLIE Rose Forge Cottage, Newnham, Sittingbourne, Kent, ME9 0LQ
YOUNG Richard Flat 1, 128 Bedford Street South, Liverpool, L7 7DB

British Library Cataloguing-in-Publication
Data Available

© Board of Trustees of the
National Museums & Galleries on Merseyside

First published in Great Britain 1991

ISBN 0 906367 51 4